Getting Commitment at Work

A GUIDE FOR MANAGERS & EMPLOYEES

Michael C. Thomas
Tempe S. Thomas

"The lessons in this book are so useful I intend to keep it close at hand."

Commitment Press
Chapel Hill, NC

GETTING COMMITMENT AT WORK
A GUIDE FOR MANAGERS AND EMPLOYEES

Published by Commitment Press
P.O. Box 2363
Chapel Hill, North Carolina 27515-2363

Printed in the United States of America

Publisher's Cataloging in Publication Data

Thomas, Michael C.

GETTING COMMITMENT AT WORK
   A Guide for Managers and Employees
    1. Employee participation
    2. Supervision
    3. Employee selection
    4. Staff development
   I. Title
   658.3152   89-90271
   ISBN 0-9623266-0-7

A BARD PRODUCTIONS BOOK
Editing: Alison Tartt
Cover Design: Suzanne Pustejovsky
Text Design and Production: Mary Ann Noretto
Composition: Graphic Express, Austin, Texas

Contents

Acknowledgments

This book is our tribute to the many committed employees and managers who have shared their experience and wisdom with us.

We extend special recognition and thanks to the people who reviewed the manuscript and gave us their invaluable suggestions and enthusiastic support: Ray Bard, Bard Productions; Linda Barnes, Branch Banking and Trust; Chip Bell; Frank Brown, President, Market Search; Hal Brown, President, Adele Knits; David Cruickshank, Vice-President, State Capital Insurance Co.; Paula Caldwell, Human Resources Consultant; Fara Faramarzpour, Polaroid Corporation; T. C. Godwin, President, T Mart Food Stores; David Hale, Easco Hand Tools; Larry Layton, DuPont Canada; Patti Murray, The Record Bar; Ed Ormsby; Marian Ruderman, Center for Creative Leadership; Rich Ruhmann, President, Ruhmann Associates; Bill Smith, North Carolina State University; Fran Tomlin, North Carolina Department of Administration; Don Woodward, Hoechst-Celanese; and Bob Wooten, Chairman, Brown-Wooten, Inc.

We also wish to express our appreciation to Mike's colleagues at Farr Associates. Thanks to Dr. James Farr for his commitment to Mike's professional development and to Pat Sims and Cary Root for their friendship and support along the way.

Comments on *Getting Commitment at Work:*

"This down-to-earth guide accurately depicts commitment as a shared responsibility. It covers the management of commitment from the hiring interview on. My advice—read it carefully, then give your employees and your boss a copy!"

Howard Denmark
Internal Consultant, CIBA-GEIGY Corporation

*"The one thing that will mean success in the convenience store industry is employee commitment. **Getting Commitment at Work** is right on the money. It is useful for executives, middle managers, and employees."*

T. C. Godwin
President, T-Mart Food Stores

". . . describes the impact of the human system gone awry, and more importantly, how it can be prevented. Should be mandatory reading for all managers in the search for world class performance."

J. David Hale
Operations Manager, Easco Hand Tools, Inc.

"Involvement and complete communication are two of the greatest motivating factors known to get total commitment in the workplace. This book is a step-by-step procedure on how to do just that."

Wes Matthews
Manufacturing Manager, Milliken and Company

"It is truly a handbook. It concentrates on how to do it rather than philosophy or theory . . . the type of book which is not just read but is reviewed and re-read to prepare for specific situations."

Byron E. Hodnett
President, First Union National Bank of Florida

"This book is a needed tool in management training. The content is excellent, clear, concise and extremely helpful."

Anne P. Hyde
President, The Hyde Group, Inc.

*"**Getting Commitment At Work** is especially timely for the 1990s. Never before have organizations, both public and private, had to face the workforce staffing and productivity challenges which this decade poses. The Thomases provide highly prescriptive information for meeting these challenges."*

S. R. Dole
Executive Vice-President,
7-Eleven Stores Group, Southland Corporation

"This book will be useful for anyone in the workplace—supervisors and employees alike. Its conversational style makes it seem more like attending a workshop than reading a book."

W. Marsten Becker
President, McDonough Caperton Insurance Group

". . . a manual for helping new supervisors learn how to handle their responsibilities and take charge of their own advancement."

Marian N. Ruderman
Behavioral Scientist, Center for Creative
Leadership

"An invaluable guide for executives and project managers in the construction industry."

Bobby Myrick
President, Myrick Construction Company

". . . the essence of what any employee and employer needs to know about people and relationships. Since most of us are both employees and employers, it has double impact."

Larry Layton
Technical Manager, DuPont Canada

"Should be required reading for all experienced managers, new supervisors, and new employees. It is more of a working manual than a book. I'll keep a copy in the left drawer of my desk."

Fred Crisp
Vice-President, Sales and Marketing
News and Observer, Raleigh, NC
President, International Newspaper
Advertising and Marketing Executives

Introduction

> "Commitment begins the moment a manager and a prospective employee shake hands. It either grows or diminishes through your daily actions and interactions."

Getting Commitment at Work is not about quality, productivity, or corporate competitiveness. Nor is it about management programs, business strategies, or leadership styles. A number of excellent books are already available that focus on corporate and management successes.

This book is about something that is far more fundamental. It is about getting the commitment of people at work. This is not a book for the executive's library. It is a working guide to help working people lay the foundation for a satisfying and successful work life.

We wrote this book because working people at all levels, from senior managers to first-line employees, have told us that lack of commitment is their biggest frustration.

Managers have difficulty finding qualified people who will put in an honest day's work. They struggle with trainees who expect privilege and responsibility without first buckling down to master the basic mechanics of their jobs. They face resistance, sabotage, and turnover when business growth necessitates long hours, operational changes, and the hiring of new employees with specialized expertise.

Employees complain just as bitterly about their managers' lack of commitment. They feel cheated when the reality of their jobs barely resembles the glowing pictures that were painted in employment interviews. They face the frustration of trying to perform well in spite of inadequate guidance and support during training. They resent it when job security and promotions are lost to outsiders with less experience but better credentials.

The specifics vary, but the underlying belief is the same: "My boss, my employees, or both don't care about me or the success of this company." Who cares? Sometimes it appears that no one does. We wrote this book because it doesn't have to be that way.

Getting Commitment at Work is about how to meet the basic challenges that create—or kill—individual success, commitment, and satisfaction at work.

Managers face the challenges of finding good employees, training them to do the job, and developing them to assume larger responsibilities.

Employees face the challenges of finding a good job, learning how to do it well, and developing the skills and support needed to move up in the company.

We focus on hiring, training, and development because these are the critical processes that create people's initial and enduring beliefs about whether their employees and managers are committed to them. Those beliefs, in turn, largely determine the level of commitment that people will give to their managers and employees. Thus, either a vicious cycle of conflict or a positive bond of mutual commitment is established. This book provides specific step-by-step action plans for creating a positive bond.

Part One focuses on hiring. Chapter Two describes how managers and applicants can lay the foundation for mutually supportive relationships. Chapter Three describes how to establish mutually satisfactory employment agreements. Chapter Four describes how to pave the way for acceptance and support of new employees in the work group.

Part Two focuses on training. Chapter Six describes how managers and employees can make "basic training" as efficient and effective as possible. Chapter Seven illustrates how to expand trainees' understanding of their jobs from a narrow focus on the job description to a broader perspective on "the big picture." Chapter Eight outlines how to remove the training wheels by developing self-responsibility and independence.

Part Three focuses on development. Chapter Ten describes how managers and employees can develop the skills needed to handle growing responsibilities. Chapter Eleven explains how to facilitate and build support for change and growth. Chapter Twelve presents strategies for creating enduring commitment that will withstand the tests of change and time.

Each part of the book begins with a scene at Progressive Enterprises, a successful, moderate-sized company that is not unlike the settings where most of us spend our work lives. The main characters are Ann, a newly hired administrative assistant; Marilyn, the administrative manager; and Jack, the vice-president and primary developer of Progressive's growing business.

The scenes illustrate the ways in which managers and employees unintentionally undermine the commitment they are trying to create. Although the scenes are fictitious, they are based on the reality that many of us experience more often than we would like. In the chapters following each scene, we explore the conflicts and misunderstandings between Ann, Marilyn, and Jack, and outline how you can avoid similar problems in your work life.

In order to get the most out of this book, there are three important guidelines that you must follow.

First, we ask you to accept the basic assumption that most people really do care and to act as if they did. We ask you to do this because people will conform to your expectations and beliefs about them. In order to break out of a cycle of conflict and establish a positive bond of mutual support, you must begin by believing that you already have the commitment that you want.

We believe that the problem is not lack of commitment. The problem is that we often neither recognize nor express commitment very effectively. We wrote this book to help you communicate your commitment in ways that your employees and managers can understand and appreciate.

Second, we ask you to read the entire book. This book is unique because it is not for managers only, but for any working person who wants greater satisfaction, success, and commitment at work. The scenes introducing each part of the book are written from the perspective of both managers and employees. Each chapter includes separate recommendations for managers and employees. We wrote from this dual perspective so that you could get the greatest possible benefit from this book.

With the exception of first-line employees and business owners, every working person is both a manager and an employee. Supervisors want commitment from the workers who report to them as well as from the middle managers to whom they report. Reading all of our recommendations will help you be more effective as both a manager and an employee, and will also help you better understand the needs and perspectives of your managers and employees.

Finally, we ask you not only to read this book but also to share it. Sharing this book with your managers and employees sends a strong positive message about your commitment to them and your belief in their commitment to you. Commitment grows when people work together. The guidelines in this book will have the most powerful impact when you, your managers, and your employees join together to make them work.

PART ONE

Hiring

1.

"The Perfect Match"

Ann was so excited about her new job at Progressive Enterprises that she hardly slept the night before her first day at work. Executive assistant to the vice-president! This was the job of her dreams after ten years in a dead-end job as a typist at Consolidated. Ann felt lucky to land an interesting job with a well-managed, growing company.

Ann intended to do well in her new job. She knew she could do the work, and she was proud to have met Progressive's high standards. Marilyn, the administrative manager, had really grilled Ann in the first interview. Ann felt uncomfortable with Marilyn's probing questions and skills tests. It had been a relief to escape Marilyn's interrogation and meet with Jack, the vice-president.

Ann was glad she was going to be working for Jack instead of Marilyn. He seemed like such a nice guy. Jack didn't make her feel like she was on the "hot seat" when he interviewed her. Ann knew Jack would expect a lot from her, but he made her feel confident and eager to meet those expectations. Ann liked all the things Jack shared with her about himself, the job, and Progressive. He said he cared a lot about employees. He made her job sound interesting and important.

Ann was looking forward to doing research assignments, making travel arrangements, and, at long last, being freed from the tedium of typing all the time. She couldn't wait to have her own office. Most of all, she wanted to join the friendly, cooperative work team that Jack had described to her in the interview.

Everything seemed perfect—the job, the boss, and the people.

7

These were Ann's thoughts and expectations about her new job at Progressive. Thus, when she arrived home from her first day of work, her husband Chuck was surprised to see the anger and disappointment in her face.

Chuck: What's wrong? What happened?

Ann: Everything—the job, the people, the boss! That jerk tricked me!

Chuck: What jerk? Jack? I thought you were looking forward to working for him.

Ann: I was, but he's not my boss. I didn't even see him today. Marilyn bossed me around all day. I never intended to work for that witch. You know how dumb she made me feel in the interview.

Chuck: Are you sure Marilyn's your boss?

Ann: Yeah, she made sure I got that straight. She acted like I was crazy to think a vice-president would supervise a support worker. It was humiliating. Jack really set me up with all that bull about caring for employees. He even lied about my salary. According to Marilyn, I won't get the salary he promised until I pass probation. Marilyn's so picky, I'll probably never pass.

Chuck: I can't believe Jack's a liar. Maybe he just forgot to mention the probation.

Ann: Sure he forgot. Just like all the other minor details he forgot to mention. I found out today that I have to pay for health insurance. With the probationary salary and the deduction, I'll be making less than I was at Consolidated. And there's more. He didn't bother to tell me I won't have an office for six months. I looked pretty dumb carrying those plants in there today. The biggest insult is that he lied about my job title. He said I was going to be his executive assistant, but Marilyn says I'm only an administrative assistant.

Chuck: Your title doesn't matter as long as you get to do some interesting work.

Ann: It matters to me—it tells people who I am! Anyway, I'm not doing any interesting work. I thought I was going to be more than a typist, but I spent the entire day typing a long proposal. I didn't even have time to take a lunch break.

Chuck: No lunch? Couldn't anybody help you with your work?

Ann: Nobody would help me. The other support people said they didn't have time to help. Yet they all managed to find time for lunch and an afternoon break. The worst part was, they acted like I wasn't even there. I don't know why Jack calls them a friendly work team, considering the cold shoulder they gave me. I was so upset I ran out of that place the minute I finished typing the proposal. I didn't even proof it, but I'm sure Marilyn will find all the errors. I don't care—nobody there cares about me.

Chuck: This doesn't sound like you. I know how much you care. You've been wanting a job like this for years. Give it some time. Things will get better.

Ann: I'm not holding my breath. I know it won't change. I've been there before. It's just like it was at Consolidated. Managers tell you what you want to hear, then use you to get what they want. I was naive to think Progressive would be different.

* * *

Marilyn was as disappointed as Ann with Ann's first day at work. She had been looking forward to some much needed support for Jack, herself, and the rest of the office staff. Marilyn had been delighted that Ann would be arriving in time to get out the Acme proposal. It was a monster to type, and without Ann, Marilyn would have ended up doing it herself.

Marilyn had been convinced Ann would be the perfect person for the job. She had thoroughly checked out Ann's skills and work habits, and had confirmed her evaluation with careful reference checks. She wanted to be sure Ann could succeed in a demanding job. After Marilyn was satisfied with Ann's qualifications, she turned her over to Jack for a final interview.

Jack focused his attention on Ann's fit with the people at Progressive. Jack knew that Ann's ability to work with him and the other employees would be as important as her technical skills. He devoted a lot of time to discussing his management style and expectations, as well as the high value placed on teamwork at Progressive. Then he listened to Ann talk about her work style and career goals. He was soon convinced that he could work well with Ann and that she would fit with the rest of the staff.

Jack closed the interview with his best sales pitch about the challenging work and great career opportunities Ann would have at Progressive. Jack liked to help Marilyn recruit good employees, and he knew he had done well when Ann accepted his job offer so enthusiastically. All in all, it looked like a perfect match.

At the end of Ann's first day, Marilyn thought it looked more like a perfect disaster than a perfect match. Ann had complained all day and had turned out some very poor work. As Marilyn sat at her desk, marking the errors in the proposal Ann had typed, Jack stuck his head in the door.

Jack: How'd it go with Ann?

Marilyn: Don't ask. Your proposal is a mess. I'll try to fix it in time for the last Federal Express pickup.

Jack: You'll have to speak with Ann about that tomorrow. Tell her that our proposals are critical—they have to be perfect.

Marilyn: I've already told her that, but she didn't seem to care. It looks like she didn't even proof it, she was in such a hurry to get out of here at five o'clock on the dot. I can't believe she's so irresponsible after all she said in the interview about her commitment to doing excellent work!

Jack: Don't jump to conclusions; it's only her first day at work. She'll turn around once you spend some time working with her.

Marilyn: I doubt that. She's not the least bit interested in working with me. She thought she was going to report to you.

Jack: How did she get that idea? I thought she knew you were the administrative manager.

Marilyn: She knew that, but that's the only thing she got straight about working here. She didn't understand the difference between reporting to you and supporting you. She kept calling herself your executive assistant and got huffy when I told her we don't go by fancy titles around here. Worse than that, she expected to start at full salary and was furious about the probationary period. How did you get her so confused?

Jack: Don't get mad at me! I thought you were going to cover all that. I can't keep those administrative details straight.

Marilyn: Well, I got them straight today. She was livid. I've never seen anybody with such a chip on her shoulder. She's only been here one day, and she has already alienated the other support workers.

Jack: I don't understand. She seemed to have such good people skills in the interview. And our people are usually so easy to work with. I was sure they would all like her.

Marilyn: No way! She put them down and acted like a prima donna. She griped about her office not being ready when none of them has one. Then she complained about having to type all day and expected them to help her. They don't know how to do the statistical tables in that proposal. They probably would have tried to help anyway, but she insulted them by saying she didn't think it was her job to be just a typist! Now they're all convinced she thinks she's too good to roll up her sleeves and do her own work. I'm beginning to think the same thing myself.

Jack: Don't make up your mind so soon. Meet with her in the morning—listen to her side. Maybe she'll surprise you.

Marilyn: I doubt it. I've seen her kind before, and I don't like them. They tell you what you want to hear in the interview, but once they get the job, it's a different story. I should have known she sounded too good to be true.

* * *

The perfect match is an elusive goal; ask anyone who has recently hired a new employee or started a new job. The applicant who looked so compatible for the job in the interview often seems to be a mismatch when the "marriage" begins.

Three kinds of commitment make up the perfect match:

- The first is strong commitment between new employees and their managers.

- The second is mutual commitment to the terms and conditions of employment.

- The third is commitment by the current work group to support new employees.

In spite of their good intentions, our friends at Progressive failed in all three areas. Their story is typical of the miscommunications that commonly accompany the selection of new employees. Ann, Marilyn, and Jack were all committed to making Ann's new job at Progressive a perfect match. Yet their actions did not communicate their caring and commitment very effectively.

It doesn't have to be this way! In the remainder of this part of the book, we examine the miscommunications surrounding each component of the perfect match and explain how managers and applicants can create the commitment that makes the perfect match a reality. Each chapter includes suggestions for both managers and applicants. It is important to read all the suggestions. Doing so will help you understand both sides of the hiring process as you go through it now. It will also help you prepare for the future time when the shoe is on the other foot. If you are a manager now, you will eventually be the applicant for an executive position. If you are an applicant now, you will eventually be hiring your own employees.

2.

Creating Commitment Between Managers and New Employees

> *"I never intended to work for that witch!"*
>
> *"She's not the least bit interested in working with me."*

The most important ingredient in the perfect match is commitment between new employees and managers.

For new employees, getting along with their managers is even more important than liking the job itself. After all, managers make work assignments and define the job. Managers are new employees' first and most important source of support. To be comfortable and effective in their jobs, new employees need to see their managers as caring and committed to their success. Ann saw her manager as critical and unsupportive. As a result, she performed miserably her first day at work.

A strong positive bond with new employees is equally important to managers. Like Marilyn, managers hire new employees because they need additional support. Fearful and resistant employees produce additional work rather than additional support. Witness Marilyn spending her day fielding Ann's complaints and working late to repair Ann's poor-quality work.

A good relationship between managers and new employees begins in the hiring process. The following suggestions to managers and applicants will help establish a positive relationship and create mutual commitment before and during the first days on the job.

FOR MANAGERS: HOW TO CREATE MUTUAL COMMITMENT WITH NEW EMPLOYEES

DISCUSS WORK RELATIONSHIPS IN EMPLOYMENT INTERVIEWS.

The most effective way to communicate your commitment to good relationships with employees is to talk about it. As obvious as this may sound, many well-meaning managers talk about everything but working together in employment interviews. Like Marilyn, you might ignore interpersonal issues, assuming that you will work well with anyone who works hard and does a good job. Not so. It takes more than ability and good work habits to create effective working relationships and commitment between you and your new employees.

Jack understood the importance of relationships and used his interview time with Ann to find out about her personal preferences in management style. He also told Ann about his own way of working with people. The predictable result was that Ann felt closer and more committed to Jack than Marilyn. Because he told her so, Ann knew Jack wanted to develop caring relationships with his employees. Because Marilyn was silent on the issue, Ann believed she was interested only in production, not people.

Show your commitment to good relationships with your employees by asking pertinent questions in interviews. Tell applicants you want to find out how to work well with them. Ask how they like to be managed and what kind of supervisory style works best for them. Then listen carefully. Follow up with additional questions such as

- Tell me about the best manager you have worked for. Why was he or she such a good manager? What would your ideal boss be like?

- What was your least favorite manager like? How did you handle the things you didn't like about him or her?

- Tell me about a disagreement you and a previous boss had. How did you resolve it?

- What kind of direction and feedback is most helpful to you? Do you prefer to work independently or with lots of guidance and instruction?

- If I become your boss, what would be the most important thing for me to say or do to support you?

These questions will open the door for honest and helpful discussion about whether you and the applicant would work well together. If you are most comfortable with independent workers and an applicant likes frequent detailed instructions and feedback, you both need to know it and to talk about how this will impact your work relationship. Exploring these issues tells applicants that you are committed to good relationships with employees. Getting the answers lets you know whether you have a fit and what you will have to work on to make the fit better.

INTERVIEW RATHER THAN INTERROGATE.

Sometimes in your zeal to locate the perfect match, you might overdo it in the interview. Afraid of making a mismatch, you may unintentionally create one by coming across like the Grand Inquisitor.

Marilyn both frightened and angered Ann with her thorough questioning. If Ann had realized that Marilyn was going to be her manager, she probably would not have accepted the job offer! As it was, Ann came to work seeing Marilyn as a critic rather than a supporter.

Marilyn's intentions were caring and supportive. Her tough evaluation was designed to select someone who could survive and thrive in a difficult job. Marilyn wanted nothing more than Ann's success.

To communicate your caring at the same time you judge whether applicants can handle the work, clearly state your intentions. Tell applicants that you are looking for people who can succeed and that to be fair to them you must probe into their knowledge and skills in required areas. Let applicants know you want them to do well instead of letting them assume that you enjoy ferreting out their flaws and weaknesses.

Giving applicants this kind of introduction to the hard assessment portion of the hiring process may not make it any easier, but it will make your potential employees feel better about you and your intentions. It certainly would have given Ann a more positive image of Marilyn and a more accurate perspective on the "grilling" she received.

CAREFULLY EXPLAIN YOUR REPORTING STRUCTURE TO APPLICANTS.

Applicants need to know who's the boss before they can make a commitment to working with that person. If applicants misunderstand the reporting structure of the company, they will feel powerless and resentful when they come to work and learn that the person they expected to work for is not their manager. They will feel, as Ann did, that they have been intentionally deceived.

Marilyn and Jack did not intentionally deceive Ann; they assumed Ann understood that support staff would report to the administrative manager. It is never safe to make such assumptions, especially when managers at different levels are involved in interviewing or when the applicant will be in direct support relationships with one or more of the interviewers. Unless reporting relationships are clearly spelled out, it is easy for applicants to erroneously assume they will be working for the most powerful (or the most attractive) person who interviews them. To find out otherwise is humiliating for the new employee and destructive to the manager-employee relationship.

Avoid assumptions and disappointments by reviewing your organization chart with applicants. If your company does not have a formal organization chart, sketch it out as you and the applicant discuss how your company is organized. If your company is growing so rapidly that your structure is constantly changing, discuss the possibilities and the flexibility required to work in such an environment. However you choose to cover it, be sure that your new employees come to work clearly understanding the following:

- To whom they report (Who will assign and evaluate their work?)

- To whom their boss reports (Will their boss's manager sometimes assign their work?)

- Who reports to them

- Who they support (people and/or departments) and what "support" means

- Who supports them (people and/or departments) and what "support" means

Specific communication to applicants about their potential place in the structure of your company creates trust and commitment. New employees must know where they fit in order to behave appropriately and work effectively with their manager and the people they support.

RECRUIT AND HIRE YOUR OWN EMPLOYEES.

Middle managers sometimes rely on their bosses or personnel recruiters to attract and close the deal with new employees. Marilyn relied on Jack to sell Ann on working for Progressive. At best, this practice weakens the relationship between you and your new employees and creates confusion about who's the boss. At worst, it puts you and your new employees in competition for the attention of the person with the real power—the top manager who hired them. That's hardly a caring relationship.

A far more effective practice is for you to use executives as advisors and sources of information to applicants. Explain to applicants the purpose of interviews with upper-level managers. Tell applicants you want them to meet with your boss so they can learn more about your company and so your boss can effectively assist you in your hiring decision. Enough said. This communicates your support of the applicant and your boss as well as your boss's support of you.

Once you reach a hiring decision, personally make the offer and do any "selling" needed. This creates commitment to you and establishes you as a legitimate authority and decision maker in the mind of your new employee. New employees naturally feel gratitude and loyalty to the person who describes and offers the job opportunity. If Marilyn had made the offer to Ann instead of Jack, Ann would have associated her positive feelings about the job with Marilyn instead of Jack!

FOR APPLICANTS/NEW EMPLOYEES: HOW TO CREATE MUTUAL COMMITMENT WITH YOUR NEW MANAGERS

DISCUSS WORK RELATIONSHIPS WITH YOUR POTENTIAL BOSS.

Just as managers should explore working relationships with applicants, it is in the applicant's best interests to do the same. An applicant can learn about a potential manager's supervisory style by asking the following kinds of questions:

- How and why do people who work for you succeed or fail in their jobs?

- What would I need to do to start and stay on the right track with you? How could I go wrong?

- How do you let your employees know what you expect of them? How do your employees know when they aren't meeting your expectations?

- Where do people go who have been working for you— promotions? transfers? another company?

- May I talk with some people who work for you now and some who used to work for you?

- What's the most important thing I could do to support you effectively?

Preface these questions by saying, "If you hire me, I will want to do whatever it takes to work well with you and succeed. I want to ask you some questions about your management style." This communicates your positive intent and keeps your interviewer from getting defensive about potentially threatening questions. It takes courage, maturity, and self-confidence to ask these questions. A caring manager will recognize this and will appreciate your careful approach to the work relationship.

UNDERSTAND YOUR POTENTIAL EMPLOYER'S REPORTING STRUCTURE.

Probably the most important information for you to acquire before accepting employment is whom you will be working for and where you fit in relation to supporting or supervising other employees. Ann incorrectly assumed she knew and was dismayed to find out differently when she reported to work.

Ask to see and discuss an organization chart. Don't be put off if the company doesn't have one; ask to talk it through. The following questions will help you construct the organization chart for yourself:

- To whom will I report? Who will assign my work and evaluate my performance?

- Whom will I support and what does that involve?

- Who will support me and what does that involve?

- Whom will I supervise?

- Who supervises my boss?

- What is the path of the work flow to and from my desk?

Keep asking questions if you get a vague answer about who will be your boss. It may mean that your potential employer has not yet decided. It may mean that you will report to someone other than the person who recruited you. Find out who that person is and be sure to spend enough interview time with that person to satisfy yourself that you can build a good working relationship with that person. You should spend more time talking with your future boss than any other interviewer because this is the person who will have the greatest influence on your job satisfaction.

APPRECIATE A THOROUGH EVALUATION OF YOUR SKILLS.

You may dislike a thorough selection process, feeling that your interviewers are trying to put you on the spot. Like Ann, you may even become hostile and defensive toward your evaluators.

Don't allow your discomfort to create a negative impression of your potential boss. Managers who thoroughly measure your job skills are acting responsibly and caringly. You need to know whether you have the skills and knowledge to handle the job so that you will not end up in a situation over your head. The appropriate way to handle a tough interviewer is to be honest and do the best you can. Take the opportunity to find out about the performance requirements for the job and your ability and willingness to meet them.

If the evaluation is favorable and you are hired, do your best to continue meeting your manager's high standards. Use your manager's critical eye to help you learn how to perform excellently. Your new manager will appreciate your commitment and will respond with commitment and respect for you. If Ann had explained to Marilyn that she would appreciate Marilyn's careful proofing of her hurried work on Jack's proposal, Marilyn would have viewed Ann and her work in a positive light.

RECRUIT YOUR NEW MANAGER.

People often think of recruitment as something that is done to prospective employees before they start work. That's partially true, but recruitment really works two ways—applicants are also "recruiting" prospective employers—and recruitment continues after you start your new job.

Your first few days and weeks on the job will set the tone of your future relationship with your manager and will largely determine the depth of your manager's future commitment to you. Next to you, your manager has the most power to make your work life satisfying and rewarding. Begin work with the objective of recruiting your new manager! You have everything to gain and nothing to lose.

To get your new manager's unqualified support, give it. Accept assignments willingly and do the best you can, assuming that your excellent performance is important to your manager even if the task appears unimportant to you. Make an effort to find out where your manager needs help and try to fill that need. Be cooperative and helpful, even if you experience some disappointments and inconveniences in your new job.

Complaining communicates self-interest rather than commitment to supporting your new manager. Ann's reaction to her disappointments was to complain about her assignment, salary, working conditions, and, worst of all, about working for Marilyn, the person whose support she needed the most. In the process she lost Marilyn's commitment and support.

3.

Creating Commitment to Employment Agreements

> *"I thought you were going to cover all that."*
>
> *"He even lied about my salary . . . just like all the other minor details he forgot to mention."*

A second important ingredient in the perfect match is mutual commitment to the basic terms of employment: pay, benefits, working conditions, job title, and job content. This is the employment contract, and it exists whether the terms are sealed with a handshake or with a legal document.

New employees show their initial commitment to fulfill the terms of the employment contract by resigning their present jobs, foregoing other job opportunities, and coming to work. Their continued commitment depends on their perceptions of how well employers live up to their end of the bargain.

In our story, Ann believed that Jack had not lived up to his promises. Her pay, title, working conditions, benefits, and the job content were all different from what she had understood and expected them to be. With each discrepancy, Ann's commitment decreased. At the same time, Marilyn's frustration level increased as she had to straighten out Ann's misunderstandings. Ann appeared to have a chip on her shoulder, to be a complaining rather than a committed employee. Marilyn and Jack appeared to be deceptive and manipulative rather than caring managers. As Ann saw it, "Managers tell you what you want to hear, then use you to get what they want."

When employment terms are mutually understood and accepted, the foundation is laid for lasting trust and commitment. The following practices will enable managers and applicants to establish an employment agreement that supports and strengthens mutual commitment.

FOR MANAGERS: HOW TO CREATE A MUTUALLY SATISFACTORY EMPLOYMENT AGREEMENT

USE A CHECKLIST OF INFORMATION ABOUT EMPLOYMENT TERMS AND CONDITIONS.

This is a simple way to make sure you cover all important points clearly, specifically, and accurately. During employment interviews, you may unconsciously focus more on getting than giving detailed information. A checklist prevents skipping or glossing over important information, particularly when more than one person is involved in interviewing. Marilyn and Jack each assumed the other was going to cover the terms of employment in detail. Neither did, so Ann came to work with incomplete and inaccurate information about her employment at Progressive.

Include the following items in your interview checklist for any candidate you intend to hire:

- **Job Content**
  Review job description.

- **Organization**
  Review organization chart.

- **Performance Expectations**
  Explain what the new employee will be expected to accomplish in the next six to twelve months. Describe your requirements for completion of training.

- **Benefits**
  Review a list of major benefits. Be sure to explain costs to employees.

- **Salary**
  Explain starting salary, schedule for reviews, ranges of increases, and commission or bonus programs.

- **Career Outlook**
  Describe possibilities, contingent upon excellent performance by the employee and successful growth by the company.

- **Employment Policy**
  Explain the terms for continued employment. Some employers prefer a policy of "at will" employment (i.e., either party may terminate employment with a specified amount of notice). Others, like Progressive, may specify an initial probationary or trial period with a more binding commitment and a higher salary after the probation. Whatever your policy, potential employees should understand it before they accept employment.

Frequently managers do not cover this information until employees are on board, afraid of revealing too much about the company to someone who may chose to work for a competitor. You must use good judgment in deciding just how much to tell prospects. A good rule of thumb is to share information that would influence your decision to accept the job if you were the applicant. Your care in communicating the terms of employment is an effective recruiting device. It shows applicants that you are committed to honest relationships with employees.

GIVE CANDIDATES A WRITTEN JOB OFFER TO REVIEW BEFORE THEY MAKE A FINAL COMMITMENT.

Typically, only candidates for upper-level professional or management positions receive written offers of employment. Yet it is at lower-level positions where misunderstandings most frequently occur about the details of employment. Giving potential employees a written offer enables them to resolve misunderstandings before they resign their current jobs and no longer have any real choice about accepting the terms. This simple courtesy goes a long way in establishing trust and commitment between you and your new employees. If Marilyn had given Ann a written offer, she could have accepted the job with full knowledge of what Progressive was committing to her.

A written offer should include

- Job title
- Starting salary

- Reporting status
- Beginning date of employment
- Employment policy

ESTABLISH REALISTIC EXPECTATIONS OF WHAT THE INITIAL JOB WILL BE.

Usually there is a gap between the time when new employees begin work and the time when they assume the full responsibilities and privileges of their positions. Every job requires some orientation and "breaking in" time, even if extensive training will not be required.

New employees' initial assignments and working conditions may be much less attractive than their expectations. Ann resented spending her first day typing, having high expectations of what her new job would be. Because she thought she was going to be more than just a typist, she felt she had been deceived about the nature of her job—a premature conclusion but one that new employees will naturally reach unless they have been told otherwise.

To avoid such misunderstandings and the diminished commitment that results from them, you must give new employees a realistic picture of what the first few weeks on the job will be like and why. We suggest holding a brief preemployment meeting at which you and your new employee can talk without the inevitable distractions and stresses of the first day at work. In this meeting discuss the following:

1. First assignments—what and why

If you are understaffed or have a backlog of work to be handled by the new employee, explain the temporary nature of the situation and the importance of the new employee's cooperation in doing this work. If the new employee must spend time doing seemingly trivial tasks in order to get the background to do the "real" job, explain the value of those assignments.

2. Working conditions—what they are now and how they will change

New employees rarely walk into a perfectly ready work setting. Furniture, supplies, and office space may not yet be available. Alert your new employees to temporary inconveniences and their expected duration.

3. Orientation and training—what and how long

While you may not be ready to discuss your entire training program, it is important to give new employees a general idea of what to expect. Telling new employees they will spend several weeks learning basic operations before they take on independent projects assures them that they really will get to handle the exciting responsibilities they were hired to do!

Usually this type of discussion takes place sometime during the few days on the job, if it occurs at all. It is too late to set expectations after someone is on the job. This is like a kid going to summer camp expecting to swim and sail, and learning upon arrival that the first two weeks will be spent cleaning out the boat house and learning safety rules. At that point, positive expectations can only be dashed, not shaped.

CONFIRM UNDERSTANDINGS AND AGREEMENTS ABOUT EMPLOYMENT TERMS BY ACTIVE LISTENING.

The best way to ensure that you and potential employees have a mutual understanding of employment terms and conditions is to listen to applicants describe what they have heard. As you cover each category on your interview checklist, pause to check the candidate's understanding of what you have covered. For example, after you have discussed the job description, you might say, "Let's review for a moment, so I can be sure that I've covered everything. Give me your understanding of the major responsibilities of this position. Are there any areas that aren't clear to you?" After outlining the job offer, you might say, "I want to be sure we're together on this. Please run through the points we have agreed on, and let me know if there's anything we've missed."

Just asking applicants whether they have any questions doesn't ensure a common understanding. People often do not realize that they don't understand, or do not want to appear dumb by saying they don't understand. If Jack had asked Ann whether she understood his job offer, she would have been sure she did, not knowing the information that was missing. The only way for both of you to know you have a mutual agreement is to have the applicant restate what you have said. Only then can you recognize and clarify misunderstandings and prevent unpleasant surprises that will undermine commitment between you and your new employee.

FOR APPLICANTS: HOW TO CREATE A MUTUALLY SATISFACTORY EMPLOYMENT AGREEMENT

USE A CHECKLIST OF INFORMATION YOU WANT TO GATHER ABOUT THE JOB.

Approach a new job as carefully as you would if you were making a major purchase, such as buying a new car. Create your own checklist of what you want to know about the job, and don't accept an offer until you have that information.

The interview checklist for managers earlier in this chapter will guide you in making your own checklist. Be aware, however, that your prospective employer may not have information organized in documents such as job descriptions to present to you. Prepare for that possibility by planning specific questions to ask as needed. Some useful questions are listed below, which you can add to or modify to fit your interests and priorities.

- **Job Content**

What's the overall purpose of this job?

What are the major responsibilities of this job?

What would an employee in this job spend the majority of the time doing?

What's the most important function of this job?

- **Organization**

To whom will I report? Who will assign my work and evaluate my performance?

Whom will I support and what does that involve?

Who will support me and what does that involve?

Whom will I supervise?

Who supervises my boss?

What is the path of the work flow to and from my desk?

- **Performance Expectations**

What do you expect the person in this job to accomplish in the first six months? How will you measure results?

Do you have written plans or goals for this position?

May we discuss them?

What training will the employee in this position receive? How long will it take? What will you expect a person to be able to do upon completion of training?

• Benefits

Detailed questions about benefits are inappropriate in preliminary interviews. Wait until prospective employers indicate an interest in hiring you before you ask these questions.

What kinds of group insurance (health, life, disability, etc.) does your company offer? What's the cost to employees?

Do you have a retirement program? What are the eligibility requirements? What are the costs to employees?

What's your leave policy? (Most employers do not provide any paid leave to employees until six months to a year after hiring.) If maternity leave is a concern, ask about it. Some people are afraid to ask, thinking the employer will not hire them if they are planning to have children. Although such discrimination is illegal, there is a risk in introducing the subject. We think it is wiser to find out before you accept the job than to risk disappointment later.

Other benefits? (If you are on a tight budget, try to find out about all costs to you, such as the "privilege" of a parking space you must pay for!)

• Salary

Again, it is inappropriate to ask questions, other than the starting salary, until you are being offered the job.

What's the salary range for the job?

How often is salary reviewed? Could you give me an average increase amount?

Is there a profit-sharing or bonus program? How does it work?

If you will be working on commission, be sure you understand how commissions are awarded and when.

• Employment Policy

What kind of job security does the company offer? What are the terms for continued employment?

How do you handle layoffs?

Is there a probationary period?

• Career Outlook

What are the advancement possibilities from this position?

You may hesitate to ask such detailed questions until you are on the job. That's like reading the sticker on a new car after you have purchased it. Your job has a lot more impact on your life than your car; it's up to you to make sure that you are getting a good deal.

Your potential employer may intend to give you thorough information about the job and conditions of employment but cannot accurately guess what is important to you. Jack covered what was important to him and assumed these were the important points for Ann. Like Ann, you will appear to have a chip on your shoulder if you wait to get the important details after you are hired and then start complaining about disappointments.

ASK FOR A WRITTEN JOB OFFER BEFORE YOU RESIGN YOUR CURRENT JOB.

Don't hesitate to ask for a written offer. An employer who will not put an offer in writing may not have been straight with you about the terms. When you receive a verbal offer, simply say you would like a letter confirming the terms so that you can review them while making a decision. This gives you a chance to be sure you understand everything correctly and shows your potential employer that you make commitments carefully and responsibly.

ESTABLISH REALISTIC EXPECTATIONS ABOUT WHAT THE INITIAL JOB WILL BE LIKE.

People usually look for a new job because they want more challenging work, more lucrative career opportunities, better working conditions, or other benefits their current work situation does not offer. As a consequence, applicants and interviewers tend to focus on the positive, exciting aspects of a job. This can lead new employees to start work with unrealistically high expectations about what the job will be like to begin with. Ann expected a private office, interesting assignments, and freedom from the typewriter—all on her first day of work!

Don't set yourself up for a fall. Employers are rarely 100 percent ready for new employees, and new employees are rarely 100 percent ready for the full responsibilities of their jobs. Prepare yourself for reality by asking about the short-term outlook for you in your job before you begin work. Ask where you will start out working. Don't be surprised if you are expected to share workspace in the beginning, and do so gracefully. Ask about what kind of work you will be doing the first few weeks on the job, and indicate your willingness to help clear out a backlog of work or do unappealing tasks that may be part of your orientation and training.

Taking the initiative to ask these questions saves you from unnecessary disappointments and from appearing negative and uncommitted when you step into the reality of a new job. Your first few weeks at work is not the time to complain about anything, particularly temporary inconveniences your manager will take care of over time.

CONFIRM YOUR UNDERSTANDINGS AND AGREEMENTS BY ACTIVE LISTENING.

Check your understandings and assumptions. As you go through the interview process, practice active listening. Periodically put what you are hearing about the job into your own words, and ask whether your understanding is correct. You may be hearing what you want to hear and not what is being said. You may simply be confused and not know it. Ann heard Jack talking about the important responsibilities of assisting an executive and translated that into the title of executive assistant for herself! She could have avoided that mistake and her other misunderstandings by active listening.

4.

Creating Commitment
for New Employees
in the Work Group

> *"Nobody would help me."*
>
> *"She has already alienated the rest of the support staff."*

The third key element of the perfect match is a commitment to support new employees by their coworkers.

New employees want to be accepted and need to be supported by their coworkers. Anyone who can remember starting a new job knows the countless ways in which new employees depend on their coworkers to help with everything from finding the rest room to avoiding the hidden land mines of office politics. One of the kindest things that caring managers can do for new employees is to pave the way for members of the work group to befriend and assist them.

Marilyn and Jack expected Ann to have no problems fitting into the support team at Progressive. When Jack interviewed Ann, he took a careful look at her people skills, cooperativeness, and orientation to teamwork. She appeared to be a good fit with the workers at Progressive.

Yet as soon as she started work, Ann offended her coworkers with her complaints and demands for assistance with her first assignment.

To her coworkers, Ann appeared arrogant and unwilling to roll up her sleeves and do her own work. In response, "the friendly, cooperative work team" that Jack had described to Ann in the interview immediately excluded Ann and refused to help her! To Ann, her coworkers appeared unfriendly, unhelpful, and uncooperative. This was hardly the good fit that Marilyn, Jack, and Ann had all expected.

The following suggestions will help managers and new employees create a more positive initiation into the work group than Ann experienced.

FOR MANAGERS: HOW TO CREATE EMPLOYEE SUPPORT FOR NEW WORKERS

INFORM ALL EMPLOYEES ABOUT JOB VACANCIES AND QUALIFICATION REQUIREMENTS.

You can begin enlisting support for new employees by first telling members of the work group about the job and its requirements. Explain the job's purpose, major responsibilities, and the skills and experience required to handle those responsibilities.

Giving employees this kind of background about a new position hastens the acceptance of the person hired to fill it. When employees understand the qualifications required, they will be less likely to resent a more skillful new person or to feel that they have been passed over unfairly. When employees understand the content and importance of the job, they will be more likely to pitch in and provide the support a new person needs to successfully do the work.

What if Marilyn and Jack had thoroughly oriented the support staff at Progressive about the new administrative assistant job? The staff would have appreciated the importance and difficulty of getting Jack's proposal completed on time and would have been more receptive to Ann's plea for help. If they had known Ann's qualifications and the full scope of the job, they might have understood her disappointment about having to spend her first day typing. They might have even been understanding enough to make Ann feel better about her assignment by admitting that they didn't have the skills to help her.

Understanding leads to appreciation, and appreciation leads to support. Inform your employees about new jobs so they can understand, appreciate, and support the people hired to do them!

INVOLVE EMPLOYEES IN RECRUITING NEW EMPLOYEES—BEFORE AND AFTER HIRING.

When you have informed employees about job openings and requirements, your employees can be excellent recruiters. Your employees know from their own experience what it takes to fit in with and succeed in your company. They are motivated to refer people with the ability to succeed since their referral's performance will reflect on them. Employees are naturally motivated to support a new person's success on the job if they played a part in helping locate that person. This will be true whether or not you hire an employee's referral as long as employees believe that all candidates were fairly considered.

The jury is still out when new employees start work. Only after they are on the job do new employees really learn what it's like to work for your company. Your "old-timers" can sell your company as a good place to work by taking an active, willing role in orienting and assisting new employees.

A buddy system is one effective way to involve employees in recruiting new workers. Ask for volunteers to be the new employee's buddy each day for the first couple of weeks at work. With a different buddy each day, new employees can gradually get to know all their coworkers and will naturally become part of the team. The day's designated buddy can greet the new employee at the beginning of each day, check from time to time throughout the day to see how things are going and answer questions, share coffee breaks and lunch with the new employee, and generally be helpful with whatever comes up. Such a system helps new employees feel at home and cared for, with the added benefit for managers that the new employee is not overly dependent on them.

It's a blessing when your employees help you locate good recruits; it's a necessity for your employees to help you keep them. Tell your employees that this is one of the most valuable contributions they can make to your company. Explain to your employees that the cost of locating and attracting good people is nothing compared with the cost of losing and replacing them.

If Ann's coworkers had understood the importance of their role in helping her fit in and like her new job and if a specific person had been assigned to be her helper, her first day could have been quite a different story. As far as Ann's coworkers knew, they had no responsibility for recruiting her, and that is exactly how they acted—with no sense of responsibility.

INVOLVE EMPLOYEES IN SELECTING NEW WORKERS.

You can create commitment to new employees, and efficiencies for yourself, by involving employees in selecting people who will be part of their work group. Inviting their participation in hiring coworkers tells your employees that you respect their judgment and preferences. It tells applicants that you are a manager who trusts and cares about employees. Employee involvement saves you the cost and trouble of finding out too late that you have a misfit in your work force. Most important, it creates support for the person your employees helped to choose.

Appropriate ways in which employees can help with hiring include screening applications, administering skills tests, and demonstrating and describing the job. With minimal training, people who do related work can screen and test applicants. With no training, employees can talk with applicants about their jobs, demonstrate operations, and answer questions about what it's like to work in your company.

Involvement in hiring gives your employees a chance to interact with applicants in the reality of the work setting, a much more effective place to assess fit with the work group than behind the closed doors of the manager's office. Jack was correct in his judgment that Ann could work well with the other members of the support team. If the support team had spent the same amount of time with Ann that Jack did, they would have reached the same conclusion and given her a much warmer reception.

GIVE NEW EMPLOYEES SOME BACKGROUND BEFORE YOU TURN THEM LOOSE IN THE WORK GROUP.

Share useful information about roles, personalities, and sensitive issues in the work group. It's helpful for new employees to know the ways in which their skills, responsibilities, and privileges differ from those of their coworkers. Tell new employees if they were selected over internal applicants and may have to deal with some bruised egos. Ann would have found it useful to know that other support personnel did not have private offices and did not possess her excellent typing skills.

New employees easily appear insensitive when they don't know what will offend their coworkers. Give new employees the background to avoid making inappropriate comments, complaints, and requests. Your new employees want to be liked and accepted; they will appreciate your support in making that happen.

FOR NEW EMPLOYEES: HOW TO GET SUPPORT FROM YOUR COWORKERS

BE POSITIVE ABOUT YOUR NEW JOB.

Don't be critical! Your coworkers will react defensively to complaints, whether your complaints are directed at them or not. This is because you are criticizing their workplace and the work with which they identify. The first step for fitting in with a new work group is to let the people know you are happy and honored to be there. Ann really was happy and excited to join the team at Progressive, but she never told them so. Instead, she let her new coworkers know how unhappy she was with her working conditions and her first assignment. Her complaints cost her the support of the group she wanted to join.

A better strategy for winning acceptance in a new work group is to behave as if you are a guest at an exclusive club. Praise the good points in the surroundings, the activities, and the people. Withhold judgments and comments about flaws. New employees are outsiders to the club. It's up to you to create an image of yourself as a person who appreciates the club and wants to be "in."

LET YOUR MANAGER KNOW YOU NEED HELP BEFORE YOU ASK YOUR COWORKERS.

New employees don't know much about the capabilities or the workloads of their coworkers. Your coworkers may also not know much about your capabilities or your work. While it is appropriate to ask for help, it is inappropriate to try to "delegate" your initial assignments to your coworkers.

Ask your supervisor how and where to get help when you think you have more than you can do or when you don't know how to do something. Managers must be told where you need help so they can line up the best person to train and assist you. If Ann had told Marilyn that the proposal was too much for her to do in one day, Marilyn would have appreciated her honesty and could have helped Ann herself.

SHOW AN INTEREST IN YOUR COWORKERS.

When you first meet your coworkers, focus on them and not yourself! Take the initiative to introduce yourself to others, and find out about them and their jobs. Ask them about what they do, whom they work for, how long they have been with the company, and what their backgrounds are. Ask them to show you their work. This not only communicates your respect for and interest in your new coworkers, it also gives you the information you need to avoid unintentionally stepping on toes. Ann would never have made her comment about being "just a typist" if she had known that the people she was talking with were primarily typists and not as skillful as Ann.

LET YOUR COWORKERS KNOW YOU RESPECT THEIR ABILITIES AND NEED THEIR SUPPORT.

Although it is unwise to ask your new coworkers to do work for you, it is smart to tell everyone you meet that you will depend on their support. Tell them that you have a lot to learn and need their valuable assistance. You'll be surprised at how helpful their response will be!

Ann made the mistake of asking for help without explaining her fear that she wouldn't be able to do it all herself. Nobody likes a know-it-all. If you try to appear completely competent and self-sufficient, your coworkers will be unlikely to give you the help you need.

Part One: Summary

Three key ingredients make the perfect match:

• Commitment between new employees and their managers

• A mutually understood and accepted employment agreement

• Commitment between new employees and their coworkers

Commitment between new employees and their managers begins in the hiring process. During interviews, managers and applicants should discuss relationship issues and reporting structures. Managers should explain the purpose of thorough interviewing; applicants should appreciate the value of a careful assessment of their skills. Finally, managers and applicants must recruit one another and communicate their willingness to be mutually supportive.

Managers and applicants can create mutual employment contracts through careful and specific communication about work content and employment terms. Both should create checklists of the information they want to cover and then practice active listening to confirm understandings. Managers should clearly state employment terms in a written job offer, which applicants can carefully review before committing to the job. Applicants and managers should discuss short-term inconveniences as well as the long-term benefits of the job so that applicants will have realistic expectations.

To create commitment between new employees and their coworkers, managers must inform employees about the position vacancy and involve employees in recruiting and hiring the person to fill it. Managers must also give new employees enough background about their peers to avoid unintentionally offending them. New employees can create acceptance for themselves by being positive about their work, showing an interest in their coworkers, asking their managers for help, and letting their coworkers know how much they need their support.

All of these actions communicate caring and enhance the commitment that new employees give and receive.

PART TWO

Training

5.

"Training Wheels"

Ann hurried to work on the last day of her probationary period. After three months at Progressive, she was eager to be released from trainee status and allowed to stand on her own.

Training had been a frustrating experience for Ann.

Anxious to prove herself capable of handling the job, Ann had impatiently suffered through weeks of observing and helping with the work of the other support staff. They were supposed to teach her the basics, but nobody had enough time to give her thorough instruction and keep up with their own work. As she was shuffled from one person to the next, Ann had learned what she could by trial and error. As a result, Ann still didn't fully understand the filing system and some of the more complicated administrative reports. Ann was confident she could get the details straight with enough practice.

Marilyn didn't seem to care how long it took Ann to learn, since she hadn't made the staff available to help Ann over the rough spots. Ann knew Marilyn was aware of her weaknesses. She inspected and corrected all of Ann's work. Ann resented Marilyn's close checking, wanting to be trusted to do it right herself. Ann rarely had a chance to finish her work before Marilyn started pointing out all the errors. Now that her training was over, Ann hoped she would be given more responsibility. She wanted to work independently and be responsible for her own results instead of having everything approved by "the Inspector."

In addition to wanting more responsibility, Ann wanted more responsible projects. The promise of important, challenging work was what had attracted Ann to Progressive in the first place. So far, Ann had spent most of her time doing routine administrative assignments. She had been allowed to do only one big project, an industry study, which she had just completed. Ann hoped Marilyn would give her other projects like the industry study so she could have a real impact on the company. She wanted to do more than handle Jack's paperwork and phone calls.

Ann assumed Marilyn was satisfied with her progress since she hadn't heard otherwise. Ann was ready to take the training wheels off, and she was sure Marilyn saw it that way, too.

While Ann drove to work planning her escape from training, Marilyn sat in her office planning Ann's performance review. Marilyn was exhausted and frustrated, having worked late the night before rewriting Ann's industry study.

Ann's training had been a frustrating experience for Marilyn.

While Ann seemed eager enough to do her job, she had dragged her feet through the necessary steps to learning it. Throughout training, Ann's attitude had been "Leave me alone and let me do my job!"

Respecting Ann's independence and abilities, Marilyn had tried to give her as much room as possible to learn at her own pace. She had allowed plenty of time for Ann to learn the ropes by observing the other support staff members. She had given Ann a complete package of resource materials to study, including everything from the employee handbook to the budget manual. She had offered her advice and assistance on Ann's industry study, a complex project that Ann had insisted she was ready to handle.

Considering all she had done to help Ann, Marilyn could not understand Ann's poor progress. Marilyn sometimes thought Ann didn't really want to learn. Ann rejected the help she needed so badly, the most recent evidence of which was her miserable performance on the industry study. Ann complained about wasting time with the other support employees when she still didn't understand Progressive's administrative systems. She resisted review of her work, yet continued to make errors. Worst of all, she had a very limited concept of the scope of her job, refusing assignments from anyone but Jack and failing to act as a cooperative team member.

Marilyn had held her criticism, hoping Ann's performance would improve over time. It had only gotten worse. Marilyn was puzzling over how to approach Ann's performance review constructively when

Ann arrived for their meeting. She decided to begin by asking for Ann's suggestions.

Marilyn: I'd like to start by asking you to tell me what we need to do to improve your training progress.

Ann: What do you mean, "improve my training progress?" I've done my time in training, and I'm ready for you to take the training wheels off!

Marilyn: You've done your time, but you haven't even mastered the basic mechanics of your job yet. Just yesterday I spent half an hour hunting through the master files for the Acme proposal while Mr. Acme waited in Jack's office. You were supposed to get Connie to explain the filing system to you weeks ago. Didn't you do that?

Ann: I did! Every time I asked, Connie told me to come back after she had finished her own work. How am I supposed to learn the mechanics when nobody will take the time to teach me?

Marilyn: You can't say nobody has taken the time to teach you. You had easy access to the entire support staff when you were observing their work. You could have learned and practiced the basics then.

Ann: Some practice! My so-called trainers were delighted to let me practice on their typing overflow, but nobody cared enough to find out what I should be learning. They made me practice on whatever they needed help with, not what I needed to learn!

Marilyn: But, Ann, you knew what kind of work you were preparing to do. You should have focused on that and let them talk with me about how to get their other work done. You can't blame your poor performance on them. Of course they didn't have time to teach you everything. That's why I gave you the resources to learn some things on your own. Take the budget reports, for example. You had the budget manual and plenty of time to study it, yet you still made mistakes in the budget reports. I expected you to know those reports inside out by now and to be ready to move on to helping with the financial statements.

Ann: That's news to me. How was I supposed to know there was any rush on the budget reports? You didn't give me a deadline. You didn't even ask me to do them until six weeks after you gave me the manual. I read it three times, but it only confused me. I've never been any good at learning from a manual. I thought I was doing well to make as few mistakes as I did.

Marilyn: How can you be so casual about your mistakes? One of the reasons you are still in training is that you are so irresponsible about your work and your learning. You let weeks go by without telling me that you did not understand the reports, and you depended on me to catch your mistakes. That's irresponsible!

Ann: It's not fair to call me irresponsible when you won't give me any responsibility. How can you criticize me for depending on you to catch my mistakes? You check everything I do before I've even finished it.

Marilyn: Reviewing your work doesn't relieve you of responsibility for learning and doing it well. I have to check your work to see how your learning is progressing. You haven't been responsible enough to let me know about your problems before you made mistakes.

Ann: You don't want to hear about my problems. I've been telling you all along that I was wasting time in training, and you haven't done anything about it.

Marilyn: Complaining about wasting time isn't responsible or helpful. I want you to think through your problems and take the initiative to suggest some solutions.

Ann: That's not the message I've been getting. Whenever I make a constructive suggestion, you shoot it down. When I tried to change the expense report form so it would be easier to understand, you told me to stop reinventing the wheel.

Marilyn: That's right. Your job is to learn the system, not to change it. You'll have plenty of opportunities to be creative after you learn your job.

Ann: You keep talking about learning my job like I haven't done anything right. I may not know all the details yet, but what about the big picture? The main purpose of my job is to support Jack. I think I've done a great job of handling his work and keeping him free from interruptions.

Marilyn: You've got a bad case of tunnel vision if you think that's the big picture of your job. You have no understanding of the impact of your actions on the big picture. For example, Mr. Acme had to call me yesterday to get information about his account. He was livid! He said he couldn't get through Jack's bodyguard. We could lose his account over something like that, and he's our biggest client.

Ann: I was only doing what Jack told me. He said not to interrupt the board meeting. So I told Mr. Acme to call back the next day.

Marilyn: Your job is to support Jack by helping clients, not putting them off. Prompt personal service is the hallmark of this company. You would know that if you had bothered to read your employee handbook or the annual report I gave you.

Ann: I skimmed over that stuff, but it didn't have anything to do with my job. Nobody ever told me I'm supposed to be a customer service representative. My job description only says I am supposed to screen Jack's calls.

Marilyn: It's time for you to stop focusing on what's in your job description and take a broader view of your responsibilities. You represent the vice-president of this company. Our clients and employees depend on your support. You act like nobody needs your help but Jack. The big picture includes more players than just you and Jack. Our fourth-quarter sales projections were late because you wouldn't give the marketing people the information they needed to prepare their report. When are you going to start acting like the important team member that you are supposed to be?

Ann: Talk to the marketing people about acting like team members! I gave them the same service they have given me. It was like pulling teeth to get them to share information for my industry study. They stalled for so long I almost didn't finish the report on time.

Marilyn: As far as I am concerned, you didn't finish the report on time. I worked past midnight last night writing the analysis that you didn't bother to do. All you gave me was a list of numbers! That wouldn't help the board at all with our strategic planning. That's another example of your tunnel vision. I gave you an important project and you missed the point altogether.

Ann: Wait a minute! I'd have to be a mind reader to see your vision of the big picture! I gave you exactly what you asked for in that report. You never said anything about analysis or strategic planning, whatever that is.

Marilyn: You never gave me a chance to tell you. As soon as I told you the numbers I needed, you insisted on doing the entire project without any help from me. You never asked any questions. You wouldn't even let me review a draft of the report.

Ann: I wanted to show you that I could handle an important assignment on my own. You always take over my work when you help. Now you've done it again. You finished that study, and I haven't learned how to do it myself.

Marilyn: Of course you don't know how to do it. You won't let me teach you. You want me to take the training wheels off before you have the skills and the vision to ride alone. We're back where we started this meeting. I'm tired of going round in circles. I've spelled out your deficiencies. I have no choice but to extend your probation for another month. I will meet with you tomorrow to discuss what you intend to do to get your training completed in that time. I hope you will come prepared to show me that you really care about learning.

* * *

Training is the most powerful tool that managers and new employees can use to build mutual commitment and create a productive, satisfying work life. Effective training strengthens commitment. To be effective, training must accomplish three goals.

First, trainees must learn to perform the basic mechanics of their jobs. Trainees who don't learn the basics will be as unhappy with their jobs as their managers are with their performance.

Second, trainees must acquire a broad enough vision of their responsibilities and impact to become effective team members and make meaningful contributions to their company. Few employees are satisfied to do a narrowly defined job. Few managers are satisfied with employees who don't have the vision to do more than the routine tasks listed in their job descriptions.

Finally, trainees must develop self-responsibility. Trainees do not want to be shackled with controls any more than their managers want to be tied up with constant inspections.

Successful training both requires commitment and creates commitment. Ineffectively managed training erodes the commitment that it could build. That's what happened with our friends at Progressive. Ann and Marilyn appeared uncommitted to the results they both wanted, and their commitment diminished as their frustrations increased. It doesn't have to be this way.

The next three chapters describe how to get the results and commitment you want through the training process. Because managers and employees alike are always "in training" or helping to train others, it is important to read the suggestions for both managers and trainees.

6.

Learning the Basic Mechanics

> *"You haven't mastered the basic mechanics of your job yet."*
>
> *"How am I supposed to learn the mechanics when nobody will take the time to teach me?"*

The first requirement for effective training is for trainees to learn the nuts and bolts of their jobs as quickly as possible.

Managers have much to gain from speedy and effective operations training. Seemingly small errors and omissions in basic training create big management headaches. Ann's misfiling cost Marilyn the time it took to hunt for an important document and the embarrassment of appearing disorganized in front of a major client.

Trainees also benefit from learning the ropes quickly. Trainees want to feel comfortable and competent in handling their routine responsibilities. Nobody likes making mistakes, even small ones. Fast mastery of the basics helps trainees feel confident and successful as they progress in their learning.

Basic training rarely goes as quickly or smoothly as managers and trainees would like. Ann's operations training satisfied neither herself nor Marilyn in spite of their intentions to the contrary.

Ann believed Marilyn didn't care how long it took her to learn the details. She saw her training as haphazard and inefficient and her trainers as indifferent. Marilyn believed Ann didn't care about learning the basics. She saw Ann as resistant to taking the necessary steps to learn. It seemed to Marilyn that Ann would not take advantage of the resources that Marilyn had so carefully provided—time to observe the other workers and to study the procedures manuals.

Managers and trainees can demonstrate their commitment and produce excellent operations training results by applying structured planning, control, and communication procedures. The following actions could have saved Marilyn, Ann, and her trainers considerable time, trouble, and frustration.

FOR MANAGERS: HOW TO CREATE EFFECTIVE OPERATIONS TRAINING

INVOLVE TRAINEES IN DESIGNING THE TRAINING PROCESS.

People learn in different ways. Some easily absorb and digest written materials. Others learn more easily by observation and hands-on training. Most people need a combination of reference material, demonstration, and practice. While your new employees may not know exactly what they need to learn, they can tell you how they learn most comfortably and quickly. Smart managers plan training to accommodate the individual's learning style. This avoids unnecessary difficulties and delays in learning.

Your trainees can tell you how they learn. Simply ask them how they have mastered new skills or tasks in the past. Useful questions include the following:

- How do you teach yourself something new? How did you learn to do your favorite hobby or sport?
- What were your best courses in high school or college? How were they taught?
- What's the most helpful workshop or training you have had? How was it conducted?

Use the answers to these questions as a guide in planning training. If a trainee tells you she learned sales skills by listening to tapes, you can predict she will respond well to oral instruction. If a trainee tells you he became a championship bridge player by studying Charles Goren books, you can give him operations manuals to study with good results.

If Marilyn had asked, Ann could have told her that she became an accomplished dressmaker by copying ready-made garments and avoiding pattern instructions because they confused her. Knowing this, Marilyn would never have expected her to learn how to complete complicated budget reports by following a manual. Instead she could have better facilitated Ann's learning by giving her completed sample reports and some dummies to practice on.

CREATE A WELL-DEFINED STRUCTURE FOR OPERATIONS TRAINING.

Typically managers structure operations training something like this: "Spend a couple of weeks working with Joe. He'll show you the ropes." End of training plan. With only this instruction, neither the trainer nor the trainee knows where to focus attention or how to most productively work together. The trainee ends up observing whatever the trainer has to work on at the time and practicing on whatever the trainer has time to explain. This is basically what happened to Ann.

Experienced employees can be excellent trainers, provided they have adequate guidance, information, and support. The best results occur when you involve on-the-job trainers in creating a structured training plan. Such a plan should outline the following:

1. Content—what trainees need to learn

As obvious as this may be to you, it is not likely to be as clear to the trainer unless the trainee is learning the very same job the trainer does.

2. Process—how trainees will be taught

Use information trainees give you about their learning styles. Discuss this with your trainers; otherwise they will do what comes naturally, which is to present information in the way that would work best for them.

3. Performance goals and measures—how you will evaluate performance

Define the standards for successful completion of training. What will indicate that each step of the training is complete? When should each step of the training be completed? Trainers and trainees need a yardstick to know when their job is done.

4. Sequence—the order of training

Careful sequencing is particularly important when several people are involved in conducting the training. A structured sequence keeps busy trainers from handing off the trainee from one person to another as time permits, rather than following a logical and complete progression of instruction. A good sequence breaks the work down into meaningful components with specific objectives for each component. The sequence of the components follows a piece of work from start to finish and allows trainees to gradually build on what they are learning. Proper sequencing may be obvious to you but not to trainers who are putting together pieces of several different jobs.

5. Schedule—the timing and length of each segment of training

Allow enough time for complete instruction while scheduling to cause the least possible disruption in normal operations. Support your trainers by recognizing the time demands of training. Arrange backup for their work or reschedule some of their normal responsibilities so they can give trainees adequate time and attention.

6. Responsibility assignment—who will teach what

Once the content, goals, sequence, and schedule of training have been determined, it is up to the manager to make sure that a specific individual is responsible for each segment of the training. Support your trainees by personally making assignments to trainers. This keeps trainees out of the awkward position of making time demands on their coworkers when they have no real authority to do so.

While this kind of detailed structuring may seem formal and time-consuming, it is the most efficient way to create the desired training results. The time saved in training will by far outweigh the time spent planning. The busier you are and the more overloaded your on-the-job trainers are, the more important it is to take the time to design an efficient plan and stick with it. Otherwise, haphazardly trained workers go on line too soon and contribute to the work overload with their mistakes.

SHARE THE TRAINING PLAN WITH TRAINEES.

Just as it is not enough to tell your on-the-job trainers to show a trainee the ropes, it is also not enough to tell a trainee to learn your administrative systems by observing experienced employees and studying manuals. Give your trainee a copy of the training plan and discuss each portion of it in detail.

Marilyn thought she had given Ann adequate information about her training by telling her about the work she was expected to learn how to do. Ann did not know exactly when, how, or from whom she was supposed to learn these things. Therefore, she learned slowly, sporadically, and incompletely. In order to successfully complete training, trainees need to know specifically what to expect from others as well as what is expected of them.

SYSTEMATICALLY MONITOR AND GIVE FEEDBACK ON TRAINING RESULTS.

Although managers frequently delegate operations training, you remain responsible for managing the training and ensuring that the intended results are achieved. Delegation without follow-up is abdication. Failure to monitor training progress is like setting up a budget with no provisions for tracking income and expenses.

It is easy to monitor training progress when you have done the kind of planning recommended above. Conduct brief weekly meetings with trainees and trainers to review progress against the training schedule and goals. Ask trainees and trainers to tell you what they are doing, how they are doing it, where they are having difficulty, and what additional assistance or instruction they would like. You can then help them as needed and praise positive results.

Never wait until the end of training, as Marilyn did, to formally review training progress. Your trainees and trainers need frequent structured guidance and feedback to stay on track and to maintain a high level of energy and commitment to learning. It is unfair to expect trainees and trainers to self-direct with only your random comments. Marilyn's apparent inattention to Ann's training communicated to Ann that her learning was not very important and led Ann to believe her progress was acceptable. Don't let your trainees make the same mistake!

Note to Managers: There are three "For Trainees" sections in Part II. In order for you to maximize the effectiveness and efficiency of your training efforts, we suggest that you give all of your trainees a copy of this book and review these sections with them. If they follow these suggestions, your time and effort in managing their training will be minimized and trainees' learning will be maximized.

FOR TRAINEES: HOW TO GET EFFICIENT OPERATIONS TRAINING

TELL YOUR MANAGER HOW YOU LEARN.

Managers know only as much about you and how to best train you as you tell them. If you aren't aware of your learning style, ask yourself how you mastered a favorite hobby or a difficult course in school. Then talk with your manager about how you learn most comfortably and efficiently.

Don't spin your wheels doing something that you know doesn't work well for you. Ann knew she had a hard time understanding detailed written instructions, yet she didn't tell Marilyn. She then blamed Marilyn's training method for her failure to learn how to do the budget reports correctly. She could have avoided the problem altogether by telling Marilyn at the time she gave her the budget manual, "I think I will learn this faster if you give me some sample reports to study and reconstruct." Ann's constructive suggestion would have effectively communicated her genuine commitment to learning.

MAKE SURE YOU CLEARLY UNDERSTAND YOUR MANAGER'S EXPECTATIONS FOR YOUR LEARNING.

This is easy when your manager has prepared a training plan. Unfortunately, many managers do not do that kind of planning. Managers are busy and, like Marilyn, they often carry the training plan around in their heads, unintentionally sharing incomplete information about their expectations. Managers will assume you understand what is expected unless you tell them that you do not.

If your manager doesn't give you a training plan, create one for yourself. Your manager will appreciate your careful and organized approach to your training, and you will avoid wasting time. Refer to the training plan outline we recommended for managers earlier in this chapter and ask the following questions:

1. What specifically do you want me to learn? (content)

2. How will I learn it? What resources will I use? (process)

3. How will I know when I've mastered it? When do you expect me to be proficient? (performance goals and measures)

4. What's the best order for learning all of this? What are your priorities for my learning? (sequence)

5. How long should I spend on each part of my training? When is the most convenient time to work with my trainer(s)? (schedule)

6. Who will teach me what? Will you let them know that they are supposed to do this and when? (responsibility assignment)

You may need to repeat these questions many times during the course of your training. The less of a planner your manager is, the more often you will need to ask. These questions may be threatening if your manager is disorganized. You can disarm your manager with a warm smile and reminders that your intention is to make training as efficient and effective as possible for both of you. Your questions will help your manager get organized and will show your commitment to learning your job.

FOLLOW UP ON THE LOOSE ENDS OF YOUR TRAINING.

Even with the best-planned training, you and your trainers will still have interruptions and other responsibilities to juggle with training. Unless you follow up, important parts of your learning may fall through the cracks, and you may hear the same thing Ann did from her angry manager, "Why haven't you learned the master files yet?"

Sometimes you will need your manager's help, but often you can keep your training running smoothly and on time through your own organization and initiative. Remind your trainers when they haven't covered something completely or when you don't understand something fully. You are more likely than they to remember where you left off and what you still don't know. Usually you will get the help you need when you communicate specifically what you need to learn.

Be both assertive and flexible about scheduling a follow-up time. Instead of letting Connie put her off with some indefinite time, Ann could have gotten better results by saying, "I understand you are very busy. Tell me when this week would be most convenient for you to show me the files, and I'll work my schedule around it." Set a specific time and a specific date to cover a specific part of your training.

If your trainer still puts you off after you explain what you need and attempt to schedule a follow-up time, consult your manager. Ask your trainer to meet with you and your manager to decide how to adjust your training schedule or your trainer's workload. This problem-solving approach avoids blaming and focuses on what you all want—efficient, effective training for you.

CAREFULLY MONITOR AND REPORT YOUR OWN TRAINING PROGRESS.

Whether or not you have a written training plan with specific goals, you can and should track your own progress. Keep a log of your activities and accomplishments. Give it to your manager for review and feedback once a week. Tell your manager what you have been doing, what you are learning, and what you need more help with. Then ask your manager whether your progress is satisfactory, what you should do to improve, and what you should do next. This helps your manager quickly review your progress, shows your commitment to learning, and saves you from unpleasant surprises when your manager initiates a formal evaluation of your work. Ann did not do this, only to discover that what she thought was the end of her training period was only the beginning.

7.

Learning Purposes: "The Big Picture"

"You've got a bad case of tunnel vision if you think that's the big picture of your job."

"I'd have to be a mind reader to see your vision of the big picture!"

The second goal in training is for trainees to make the transition from mastering the mechanics to understanding the meaning and impact of their work. Before they can become fully effective and committed employees, trainees must be able to accurately see themselves and their roles in "the big picture."

When trainees do not acquire this larger vision, their effectiveness and commitment will be underdeveloped. Consider this example. An enthusiastic sales trainee believes his mission is to make as many sales as possible. He breaks sales records by committing to unrealistic delivery deadlines and extending credit to financially unstable customers. Costly production and collection problems result because he does not understand the larger goal of company profitability. The trainee's enthusiasm and commitment will decline when he is criticized for his sales "success." At the same time, the trainee's manager will be less inclined to support a trainee who appears uncommitted to company success.

This was the situation with Ann and Marilyn. Ann's actions were consistent with her narrow view of her job. She believed that her mission was to support Jack. To this end, she zealously guarded his time and gave low priority to helping anyone but Jack. Ann believed the purpose of the industry study was to collect data, and she followed

Marilyn's instructions on data collection to the letter. Ann could not understand Marilyn's criticism of her good work. Marilyn could not understand Ann's uncooperativeness with coworkers and customers and her failure to grasp the purpose of an important project. Once again, Ann and Marilyn experienced each other as uncommitted.

To avoid this kind of misunderstanding, managers and trainees must develop a shared vision of the big picture. The following suggestions will help you create such a vision by carefully exploring the meaning, purposes, and impact of trainees' work.

FOR MANAGERS: HOW TO HELP TRAINEES SEE THE BIG PICTURE

SPECIFICALLY CONNECT TRAINEES' JOB RESPONSIBILITIES WITH THE PURPOSES AND GOALS OF YOUR COMPANY.

This is the first step in helping trainees see the big picture. It involves more than just giving trainees their job descriptions and other literature to read about the company. A job description tells trainees what to do; it rarely explains why. Other documents, such as employee handbooks, budget narratives, or annual reports, may describe the mission and goals of your company but may not connect the achievement of those goals to specific jobs or work units. Unless you guide trainees in making the leap from their job duties to the mission of your company, your trainees will tend to operate within the narrow confines of their job descriptions, sometimes at counterpurposes with the larger goals of your company.

Help trainees see the impact of their work on achieving the purposes and goals of your company by mapping out the connections as follows:

1. Start from the top, explaining the mission and goals of your company. Tell trainees why you are in business, what your company is trying to accomplish, and how you accomplish your goals. Give trainees written statements for clarification and future reference, but be sure to discuss the meaning of such statements in concrete terms. For example, customer satisfaction is a goal for most companies. Make that goal meaningful to your trainees by

explaining exactly what your company does or produces to create customer satisfaction. Is it your personal service? Is it your flexibility in creating custom products or services? Is it your responsiveness to customer problems? Is it the timeliness of your deliveries? Is it your competitive pricing? Is it the uniqueness of your service? The more specific and detailed your explanation of your company's mission, goals, and methods for reaching those goals, the more trainees can contribute to meeting those goals.

2. Next, describe the activities and purposes of your work unit as they relate to supporting the mission and goals of your company. Again, be specific and concrete. Suppose your unit produces widgets to certain specifications within a certain time frame. Explain how the widgets are used by your customers. Explain why the specifications are important and what happens if specifications are not met. Explain how the schedule is set, what happens if it is not met, and what speeds and slows production. Whatever the activities of your work unit, concretely describe the purpose of the work and its impact on your company's success.

3. Finally, discuss your trainees' specific job responsibilities as they relate to the goals of your work unit and of your company. At this point, let your trainees take the lead in the discussion. Ask them to describe how their work impacts the achievement of your work unit's goals and your company's goals. Ask the trainee who turns the screw in the widget to tell you why the fit is important, how the widget is used, and how he or she supports your work unit and your company by tightening the screw properly. As you listen, you can clarify and add to the explanation until your trainees fully understand the meaning and impact of their work.

The sooner you have this discussion with trainees, the better. Trainees cannot be fully effective or committed to achieving their purposes until they know what their purposes are. Ann saw "support the vice-president" and "screen the vice-president's phone calls" in her job description. To Ann, that meant "keep him free from interruptions." Had Marilyn explained Progressive's goal of customer satisfaction, Jack's critical role in responding to customer needs at the executive level, and Ann's role in supporting Jack's purpose by helping customers when Jack was unavailable, Ann would have more accurately interpreted and performed her job tasks.

EDUCATE TRAINEES ABOUT OTHER WORK UNITS AND EMPLOYEES.

In addition to understanding the importance of their own job responsibilities to your company's success, trainees must also learn to appreciate and support the responsibilities and purposes of employees in other work units. Don't assume this will happen naturally. What will happen naturally is that trainees and other employees will do what their manager tells them is important and will resist honoring "unauthorized" requests. The first step toward creating teamwork is to tell trainees that their support to other employees is important, necessary, and expected.

The second step for creating mutual appreciation and support among trainees and other employees is to involve employees from other work units in training. Set up brief meetings between trainees and a representative from each work unit in your company. Ask the work unit representative to explain the activities and purposes of his or her group. Describe the trainee's job if, like Ann's, it is a new position. After the meeting, the work unit representative can introduce trainees to other people in the unit and demonstrate operations. If appropriate, arrange for trainees to attend a staff meeting of the unit. This gives trainees a complete orientation to your company. It also sends a clear message from you and the cooperating managers of other work units that everyone's work is important and that all employees are interdependent.

Ann never received this kind of orientation. In her ignorance, she had little motivation to help the marketing director or anyone else but Jack. The marketing people had equally low motivation to help Ann, not understanding what her job was all about. Educate your trainees about other work units and the employees in them so that they can be committed to supporting one another and the larger goals of your company.

DISCUSS THE PURPOSE OF SPECIAL PROJECTS BEFORE EXPLAINING THE MECHANICS.

It is just as important for trainees (or any employee) to understand the purpose of special project assignments as it is for them to understand the purpose of their routine job responsibilities. It is more difficult than you may think to create this understanding. Trainees are often so eager to prove they can handle a big project that they skip getting the background necessary to do it well! As soon as you start talking about *what* to do you have lost trainees' interest in the more important, but less exciting *why*.

Introduce a special project assignment in the same order we recommended for connecting trainees' job responsibilities with your company's mission. Begin with the big-picture implications of the project. Why does the project need to be done? Who will be the user of the final product? What is the user looking for? What are the expected results? How will the project results be applied? And so on, until trainees understand the purpose and expected results of the project.

In Ann's situation, Marilyn should have started by telling her that the board of directors had requested an industry study because they wanted to know how certain market conditions would affect their long-range plans for service expansion. Ann would have quickly understood that an industry study is more than a collection of numbers about market conditions. By telling Ann what to do first, Marilyn generated commitment to the mechanics of the project rather than the results. Avoid this problem by explaining *why* first and then *what* is involved in a project.

ALLOW TRAINEES TO COMPLETE THEIR OWN PROJECTS.

Nothing tempts the time-pressured manager more than to personally wrap up an incomplete project and then give trainees feedback on the inadequacy of the work. You may justifiably fear that if your trainees were so far off the mark to begin with, they will be unable to meet the deadline and produce acceptable results. That is a self-fulfilling and self-perpetuating prophecy. It's self-fulfilling because your trainees lose the chance to succeed. It's self-perpetuating because your trainees learn to depend on you to take care of inadequate work. Trainees who are not allowed to complete their own projects will never get the point. Often the only way to get the point is to have to think it through to the end.

You can advise your trainees and ensure you get the desired results without taking over trainees' work. Simply set up two or three required progress review points and allow some extra time for rework in your deadline. In your reviews, advise trainees on the appropriateness and direction of their work to date, but don't do the work for them. In your final review, go over the entire project as the user(s) would, and send your trainees back to the drawing board if necessary. If you have allowed an extra week or so before your deadline on the project, your trainees will have time to make the needed adjustments.

FOR TRAINEES: HOW TO GAIN AN ACCURATE VIEW OF THE BIG PICTURE

LEARN AND SUPPORT YOUR COMPANY'S PURPOSES AND GOALS.

Actively seek information about your place in the big picture of the company you have joined. You will find that there's a lot more to performing your job effectively than just doing what's written in your job description. Start by asking your manager what you can read to help you understand your company's mission, goals, and strategies. Good sources of information include annual reports, advertising brochures, policy manuals, and employee handbooks. Managers often include these materials in orientation packages for new employees, and new employees are often so busy learning how to do their jobs that, like Ann, they quickly skim the documents and get back to work! Show your commitment to understanding and supporting the goals of your company by carefully reading your orientation materials. Then initiate a discussion with your manager about how you see your job fitting in with the goals of the company.

This will give you the perspective to be an effective as well as a technically competent employee. When you show an interest in the big picture, your manager will see you as a valuable and committed employee. You can further enhance this positive image by asking for more. What are the goals of your work unit? How can you help achieve those goals? Is there a budget or long-range plan you can review that will help you understand what your company and your work unit is trying to accomplish? Keep asking questions until you have a clear picture of how your work supports the purposes of your work unit and your company.

LEARN AND SUPPORT YOUR FELLOW EMPLOYEES' PURPOSES AND GOALS.

Be political in a positive sense by getting to know and helping people in all departments of your company. While your first priority in training is understanding the purposes and mechanics of your own job and work unit, you must also become a supportive team member of the total company.

Everything you do connects with someone else's work, often someone in a different area of your company. Explore your connections with other people in your company and do everything you can to make those connections positive and constructive. If your manager does not arrange a formal orientation to other people and other work units as part of your training, do it yourself informally. Make every contact with people in other departments an opportunity for developing cooperative relationships. Here are three ways to do this:

1. Whenever possible, personally deliver work that goes to other departments, introduce yourself to the recipient, and find out what that person does and how your work is connected. Do the same when people bring information or work to you.

2. Respond positively to requests for assistance from other employees. Show an interest in their work and how you can help. If the request will mean a time-consuming project for you, let the person making the request know that you are willing to help and that you will check with your manager about arranging the time to get it done.

3. When you ask for help from people in other departments, be sensitive to their workload demands and priorities and fully explain what you need and why. This approach establishes a network of support between yourself and all the other employees in your company. It shows your manager that you are a committed team player. If Ann had learned more about other departments and had been more helpful toward the other employees at Progressive, she would have received much more support from them and from her manager.

MAKE SURE YOU UNDERSTAND THE PURPOSE AND INTENDED RESULTS OF SPECIAL PROJECT ASSIGNMENTS.

Most trainees jump at the chance to do a special project—something outside the bounds of their routine job responsibilities, something that will enable them to show their stuff and have a visible impact on the company. Temper your eagerness to act with careful attention to understanding the purpose of what you are being asked to do. This is the only way to keep yourself from making Ann's mistake of taking the right steps but arriving at the wrong destination.

When your manager asks you to do a special project, your first response should be "Great! What's the purpose of this project?" instead of "Tell me what to do." Here are some important questions to ask:

1. What results do you want from this project? Do you want information, analysis, recommendations, plans, or what?

2. Who will receive the project report (or other product)? How will they use it? What are their concerns/priorities? How much detail/summary will they want? May I talk with them about it?

3. What resources should I use? Has anyone done a similar project that I can review?

Ann could have applied these questions to her industry study and done a more effective job. You can apply them to any project assignment, whether or not a written report is involved. Your thoroughness in understanding the assignment will demonstrate your commitment to doing well and will make your work easier.

SEEK AND ACCEPT YOUR MANAGER'S GUIDANCE AND FEEDBACK BEFORE YOU COMPLETE PROJECTS.

You can get on the right track with special projects by following the recommendation above; you will stay on the right track by sharing your plans and progress with your manager before you reach the end of the line. When you hide your work and resist help, your manager can only assume you are either a mind reader or that you don't care enough to get the help you need. This is how Ann appeared to Marilyn, and Ann was ironically correct in her statement that she would have to be a mind reader to see Marilyn's vision of the big picture!

The following steps will help ensure your success with special projects:

1. Tell your manager how you intend to carry out the project before you do anything. Summarize the major steps and intended results of each. If you are planning a lengthy or complex project, give your manager a written outline. This will help you think through what you need to do and will help your manager more easily give you direction.

2. Agree with your manager on when and how you will get feedback on your progress. Ask your manager to describe what is expected at each review point.

3. Accept and act on your manager's valuable critique with appreciation, not defensiveness and resentment. Assume you will have to do some revision and allow time for it. Revision is sometimes the only way you can get an accurate vision of your work! Your willingness to revise your work shows your commitment to learning and doing it right.

8.

Learning Self-Responsibility

> *"One of the reasons you are still in training is that you have been so irresponsible about your work and your learning."*
>
> *"It's not fair to call me irresponsible when you won't give me any responsibility."*

The ultimate goal in training is to develop self-responsibility. Managers and trainees alike face a real dilemma in meeting this goal because of the nature of the training process.

During training, managers must limit trainees' authority and carefully inspect their work until trainees have learned the system and demonstrated the competence and responsibility to work independently. In effect, managers assume responsibility for trainees' work until trainees have the experience and knowledge to be self-responsible.

Trainees, on the other hand, are necessarily dependent on their managers and trainers to teach and closely supervise them. They don't yet know enough to be independent and self-directing, however much they may want to be.

As a result, the training relationship frequently fosters passive dependence and irresponsibility. Managers direct and correct; trainees do as they are told. "Good" trainees accept controls, follow directions, and don't try to change the system. Yet the ultimate goal of training is to produce employees who act independently, exercise self-control, and initiate constructive suggestions.

Ann and Marilyn missed the goal of developing Ann's self-responsibility. Marilyn's continual inspections, rejection of Ann's suggestions, and failure to respond helpfully when Ann reported problems with her training all told Ann that Marilyn did not want her to be responsible. Ann's continuing failure to do her work correctly, her misspent energy in trying to change what she did not yet understand, and her griping about wasting time in training all told Marilyn that Ann was irresponsible.

The following actions would have helped Ann and Marilyn communicate and build self-responsibility within the necessary bounds of training. Our recommendations involve careful communication about the purpose of training controls and focus on sharing controls and learning the problem-solving skills that are the foundation of self-responsibility.

FOR MANAGERS: HOW TO DEVELOP SELF-RESPONSIBILITY IN TRAINEES

COMMUNICATE YOUR EXPECTATIONS FOR SELF-RESPONSIBILITY DURING TRAINING.

Tell trainees that self-responsibility and independence are the ultimate goals of training. Specifically explain how to demonstrate self-responsibility during training.

This is difficult to communicate because trainees typically think of training as something that is done to them before they are given responsibility or held accountable for their work. In order to give trainees a new way of looking at their responsibility in training, you must clearly and specifically communicate the following ideas and expectations:

1. Self-responsibility begins in training. The trainee's first responsibility is to learn. You and your on-the-job trainers will support learning by providing the necessary information and resources. You expect your trainees to actively seek and make the best use of the resources provided.

2. You expect trainees to demonstrate responsibility for learning by initiating actions to help themselves learn. Responsible trainees share information that will help you design the most efficient and

effective training process. They make sure they understand and meet your expectations for their training (content, process, goals, sequence, schedule, and responsibility assignment). They take the initiative to followup on the loose ends of their training plan. They track their progress and keep you informed about where they are. In other words, they take the steps we recommended to trainees for learning the mechanics.

3. Inspection and other controls you exercise on trainees' work are temporary limits intended to help trainees learn. Your controls are not motivated by lack of trust or confidence in trainees' abilities. Your controls are motivated by your commitment to trainees' success. You expect trainees to demonstrate responsibility by using controls to help them learn their work well enough so that the controls are no longer needed.

4. You expect trainees to concentrate first and foremost on learning the system as it is. Their ability to change and innovate effectively will depend on how well they understand the current system.

Repeat. Specifically communicate to trainees that self-responsibility is the ultimate goal of training. Clearly explain how to demonstrate and develop self-responsibility in training. And repeat the message until your trainees fully understand and demonstrate their understanding with self-responsible actions!

Don't assume that trainees know this already. Ann didn't. Most people have been taught in school and previous jobs to be passive, dependent learners and to let their bosses and instructors bear the full burden of planning, executing, and evaluating training. You must spell out what it means to be a responsible learner. It may well be the first time your trainees have heard it!

USE SUGGESTIONS FOR CHANGE TO HELP TRAINEES LEARN THE SYSTEM.

Although trainees should focus first on learning the system as is, in the long run you want trainees to become responsible employees who question the status quo and suggest improvements. When you impatiently dismiss suggestions, trainees get the unintended message that their ideas are not wanted.

There are two ways in which you can simultaneously encourage learning and innovation. The first is to assign trainees to a committee or task force that will analyze and recommend improvements in a work procedure. Trainees will provide a fresh perspective and insight that you and your experienced employees may no longer have. More important, trainees will thoroughly learn the operation while they also pick up valuable analytical skills, meet and learn how to work with others in the organization, and get the message that you support constructive change.

The second way to demonstrate your support for responsibility and initiative is to let trainees follow through and test their "better ideas." Investigating whether a proposed change will or will not work requires trainees to look closely at how the system does work. When trainees find out for themselves, instead of being told that a suggestion is not feasible, they accept the verdict and see their managers as supporting responsible suggestions.

Ann would have felt better and learned more if Marilyn had thanked her for her suggested revisions to the expense report form and given her the guidance she needed to check out its workability.

USE COMPLAINTS TO TEACH PROBLEM-SOLVING.

Most trainees will come to you untrained in problem-solving. They will have been "trained" through past experience to either ignore problems until the manager notices them (don't make waves), or to tell the manager and let the manager fix them (don't make mistakes). Either way, you must retrain employees to responsibly look for, confront, and solve problems.

Problem-solving training should begin the first time a trainee comes to you with a complaint. Resist the temptation to tell the trainee what to do to fix the problem or to criticize the trainee for griping. Instead, thank the trainee for telling you about the problem. Then ask the following questions and listen:

1. Tell me all about it. How frequently and where does this happen? Who is affected by this problem? What are the consequences of this problem?

2. Why is this happening? What is causing this problem?

3. What do you want to be different? What would be happening if you didn't have this problem? How will you know the problem has been solved?

4. What are your suggestions for solving the problem? Is there more than one way to solve it? What are the pros and cons for each way?

5. What do you want other people to do to help you solve the problem? How will you get them to do that?

You may notice that all of these questions put you in the role of listener and guide rather than problem-solver. They give ownership of the problem to the trainee and responsibility for solving the problem to the trainee. There's no better way to develop self-responsible employees than helping them resolve their own problems in this fashion.

If Marilyn had used this approach with Ann when she complained about wasting time in training, she could have led her to taking responsible actions to improve her training. By criticizing Ann and ignoring her complaints, she communicated that she wasn't committed to helping her, and she taught Ann to be passive and irresponsible.

TEACH YOUR TRAINEES SELF-CONTROL.

Although managers must carefully monitor trainees' work, you do not want trainees to learn to depend on external quality controls. You can prevent this problem by teaching trainees to evaluate their own work as they learn how to do it. Here's how:

1. When presenting each new task, tell trainees what you are going to look for when you review their work. Thoroughly describe your evaluation standards and provide examples of good and poor work.

2. Talk through your first review with trainees. Explain again what your standards are for evaluating the work and how you can tell if the work meets those standards. Identify the strong points of the work in addition to the weaknesses. (Trainees don't always know what they've done right!)

3. Ask trainees to talk you through the second review. Let them tell you what's correct and incorrect and how the work could be improved. Provide additional guidance as needed.

4. Make the third review your last "training inspection." By then, you shouldn't be getting any repetitive errors, and you may get a piece of near-perfect work. If you don't, you either haven't clearly

communicated what you want or you need to make some adjustment in the training.

This approach transfers controls to trainees as quickly as possible. It requires much less management time than continuing to inspect and correct the work of irresponsible trainees. It forces you to give timely and specific feedback so that trainees can learn to critique themselves. When trainees have responsibility for monitoring the quality of their own work, they have no one but themselves to resist or defend against. Since most people are their own toughest critics, you can create self-controls and improve quality at the same time.

FOR TRAINEES: HOW TO DEMONSTRATE SELF-RESPONSIBILITY IN TRAINING

ACCEPT RESPONSIBILITY FOR YOUR LEARNING.

Of all the players involved in training, you have the greatest responsibility. You are the one who needs to learn, and only you can do it. While your manager and trainers are responsible for delivering your training, you must be a responsive and responsible learner. Approach your learning with all the initiative and determination to succeed that you would give any major job responsibility.

Read again our suggestions earlier in this chapter to managers for communicating your responsibility in training. They will tell you what you can do to demonstrate self-responsibility. In addition, remember that self-responsible trainees give credit to others for supporting their learning but do not blame others for poor results. Blaming gives the appearance of irresponsibility and blocks the way for getting the support you need. Ann had a legitimate need for more support from Marilyn and her trainers; instead she got less support because she blamed others for her problems.

FOCUS ON LEARNING THE SYSTEM.

Don't try to move the mountain until you have first climbed it. You will have a different perspective from the peak than from the ground, where your ideas may not look so good. This is not to say that you won't have valid questions and suggestions about what you are learning. Go ahead and ask, "Why do it this way?" and "Why not do it that way?" Discovering the answers will help you learn.

The responsible way to handle your ideas for improvements during training is to let your manager know what you are up to before you act. Tell your manager, "This expense report is confusing to me. Would it be a good use of my time to revise it?" This communicates your desire to contribute and gives your manager the opportunity either to explain the areas you are having trouble with or to give approval and guidance for your project. It keeps you from going off on a tangent. If you do as Ann did and make a change without checking it out first, your action may be interpreted as irresponsible, and your time may be wasted!

TAKE A PROBLEM-SOLVING APPROACH TO YOUR DIFFICULTIES.

Be honest with your manager about the problems you encounter during training and think about what you can do to resolve your difficulties on your own. A wise manager once told us that there are four kinds of problems.

The worst kind of problems are those that managers don't hear about until they get so bad they can no longer be hidden.

Barely acceptable problems are those that employees present with a complaint and no solutions: "I'm wasting time in training, and I don't like it!"

Good problems are those that employees bring to the manager with some ideas for solving: "I'm wasting time in training. People keep showing me what I already know how to do. Maybe I should give the trainers a list of what I have and have not learned so they will know what to cover."

The best kind of problems are those that employees report that they have solved! "I was wasting time in training until I suggested the support staff get together to decide how we could do it better. I told them what I needed to learn, and they each scheduled a convenient time to help me learn it. Things are going much better now."

During training you need more guidance in handling problems than experienced employees, so you may not be able to share the "best" kind of problems with your manager. Until you really know your job and your way around the company, give your manager "good" problems. Be open about your difficulties. Analyze the situation and come up with ideas about what will help. When you go to your manager with a problem *and* possible solutions, you will be seen as helpful and responsible, and you will win your manager's commitment to helping you. When you go with a problem only, you are seen as complaining and irresponsible.

ASSUME RESPONSIBILITY FOR THE QUALITY OF YOUR WORK.

As you learn, do everything you can to produce high-quality work on your own. "On your own" does not mean working without help or inspection; on the contrary, it means making full use of the resources and controls available to you so you will not produce unnecessary flaws. The easiest way to self-control is to adopt these approaches:

1. When you are learning a new task, ask for information that will help you check your own work: "How will you know when I've done this right? Can you show me a good example, and tell me what makes it so good? What kinds of mistakes will you be looking for when you check this work? Can you show me some examples of those mistakes?"

2. When you complete a new task, ask your manager or trainers if you may be present while they check it. Ask a lot of questions. Be sure you understand what is right and wrong with what you did and why. For every error you made, explain how you did the work and ask what you need to do differently so you won't repeat the mistake. Remember, you don't just want the right answer; you want to learn how to get the right answer.

3. Be your own inspector. After you understand what is expected and have been through a review with your manager, inspect your own work and strive for perfection. When you show such responsibility, your manager will be able to trust you. As long as you depend on others to catch your errors, you are giving away your responsibility. Act as if you were your final control and soon you will be.

Ann chose to give responsibility for controlling her work to Marilyn by not initiating the steps to learn how to do it right and check it before she turned it in. She thought that Marilyn would not give her any responsibility, but Ann actually gave away the self-responsibility that was hers to begin with. You can keep your responsibility and earn your manager's commitment by controlling your own work.

Part Two: Summary

Before the training wheels come off, three goals must be achieved. First, trainees must learn the mechanics of their jobs. Second, trainees must acquire the perspective to see where they fit into the big picture of the company. Third, trainees must become self-responsible employees.

Managers can help trainees learn the mechanics by fitting the training method to the trainee's learning style, creating a carefully defined structure for operations training, communicating the training plan and expectations to trainees, and systematically monitoring and feeding back training results. Trainees can help themselves efficiently master the mechanics by telling their managers how they learn, making sure they understand training plans and expectations, following up on the loose ends of their training, and monitoring and reporting on their own progress.

Managers can create a shared vision of the big picture by mapping the connections between trainees' work and the purpose and goals of the company as well as by educating trainees about the work and goals of employees in all work units in the company. Managers can help trainees successfully perform projects requiring a broader vision by explaining purposes of the project before discussing the mechanics and by allowing trainees to complete their own work. Trainees can learn to see the big picture by learning and supporting the mission and goals of the company and of other employees, thoroughly understanding the purpose and intended results of project assignments, and getting feedback on projects before the work is done.

To develop self-responsibility during training, managers should explain to trainees exactly how to demonstrate responsibility, and trainees should accept responsibility for their learning. Managers can use trainees' suggestions for changing the system to help them learn and develop the skills needed for later innovation, while trainees should focus primarily on learning the system so they can make improvements later. Managers should teach trainees problem-solving and self-control. Trainees should discipline themselves to think through problems before complaining and to be their own quality control inspectors.

Each action by managers and trainees toward removing the training wheels is an expression of caring. As trainees' skills and effectiveness grow, their commitment and their managers' commitment to them grow also.

PART THREE

Development

9.

"Growing Pains"

A year has passed since Ann's probationary evaluation. It was a challenging and successful year for Ann, Marilyn, and Jack. Ann became an excellent administrative assistant and gradually took over much of Jack's public relations work with Progressive's client base. Working long and hard, Marilyn stayed on top of the administrative overload resulting from Progressive's rapidly growing business. Jack focused on keeping the company growing, triumphantly ending the year with the acquisition of Competitive Enterprises, a regional rival.

The employees at Progressive were elated by the acquisition. Marilyn and Ann were particularly pleased, both hoping for promotions as a reward for their good work. Although they had not discussed their specific ambitions with Jack, they were optimistic. Marilyn wanted to become vice-president with total responsibility for administrative services. Ann wanted to move into sales, an interest she had developed as she became more involved in working with Jack's clients.

Two weeks after he announced the Competitive acquisition, Jack met with Marilyn to discuss her role in managing the expanded company. Jack started the meeting with an apology for having to rush. He only had fifteen minutes before leaving town to wrap up the final details of the acquisition. Marilyn wasn't surprised—Jack was always too busy negotiating deals to spend much time talking with employees. Jack praised Marilyn for her contribution to the Competitive acquisition. He told her how much he had depended on her to keep the office running smoothly without draining his time. He gave Marilyn a substantial bonus check and a big hug. Marilyn appreciated this moment of recognition, remembering the many times she had wondered whether Jack really noticed all her hard work.

After praising Marilyn, Jack explained that he needed her help now more than ever in order to successfully take over Competitive's accounts. He acknowledged that it would be too much for her to handle alone, so he was bringing in a bright young M.B.A. from Competitive's executive team to help her out. John Newman would start next week in the position of vice-president for administration. Marilyn would be promoted to assistant vice-president, reporting to John. Marilyn's first responsibility in her new position would be to teach John Progressive's administrative systems.

While Jack rambled on about the important work she had ahead, Marilyn sat silently, looking as if she were about to cry. Jack finally noticed her discomfort and reassured her that he was confident she could handle the job. Before he could say more, Ann buzzed Jack to warn him he was going to miss his flight if he didn't leave immediately. Jack patted Marilyn on the back as he rushed out of the office and said comfortingly, "I know you must feel overwhelmed by all of this. Take the week off to rest and get yourself together before John arrives. I'll be out of town until Monday, which is his first day. Spend Monday morning showing him around, and then I'll meet with both of you to discuss this further. I'm sure you'll feel better by then."

Jack got to work late the Monday after his trip. John had already arrived and was meeting with Marilyn in her office. Jack decided not to interrupt them until they were ready to meet with him. A few minutes later, John came into Jack's office and handed him a brief letter.

Jack: Are you and Marilyn already finished? How did your meeting go? What's this letter?

John: Read it and weep! You bet Marilyn and I are already finished . . . that's her resignation letter. She dropped this bomb on me the minute I walked in the door. Why didn't you warn me this was coming?

Jack: Warn you? Why didn't she warn me? I had no idea this was coming. Marilyn has been with us since we established the company. I thought she was my most loyal employee.

John: That's exactly what she said—she thought you were loyal to her. Now she thinks you betrayed her by hiring me.

Jack: That's crazy! I just gave her a big bonus and a promotion. What more did she want?

John: She wanted my job! She didn't think assistant vice-president was adequate reward for ten years of service. And she was insulted to have to teach me your systems. She didn't understand why she couldn't have the job if she was going to train someone else to do it.

Jack: Train you? You were going to be training her. She doesn't have the knowledge of the industry, the education, or the experience to do what you can. I wonder where she got the idea she was qualified to be vice-president.

John: From you! She read me your comments from her performance reviews. In every review you said that her performance far exceeded your expectations for an administrative manager and that her advancement potential was unlimited. She believes credentials are unimportant because you were always bragging about how you made it to the top without special training or academic credentials. Even I have a hard time understanding how you could lead her on like that!

Jack: I didn't lead her on. Potential and current ability are two entirely different matters. I was planning to make her vice-president in a few more years, after she had had a chance to learn from you and attend the management development program at the university. I've been so busy with business development I haven't had time to invest in anyone's professional development, not even my own. I moved up the hard way, but I can't make this business grow any bigger without more professional know-how in the management team. I hired you to cover for my own weaknesses as well as those of my staff. Nobody here knows how to manage a company the size we are becoming.

John: I can see that. Who have we got to take over for Marilyn?

Jack: Nobody here comes close to knowing what Marilyn does; she set up our administrative systems. Ann, my administrative assistant, can help a lot, though. Marilyn trained her.

Johnny: Anything will help at this point. I have to move quickly on this. We've only got six weeks to install the computer system. Is Ann ready to become administrative manager?

Jack: No, she's not ready, and even if she were, I'm not. One of the many reasons I couldn't move Marilyn up to vice-president was that she had not trained Ann to be a manager. On top of that, nobody else here can handle the work that Ann does for me. Without Marilyn, I'll need Ann's help as much as you do. You can use her some, but not full time. Ann's not the only person who can assist you. There's a sharp guy in customer service named Harry. He was involved in computerizing services for his former employer. He might be able to help you . . . but he may be going on vacation soon.

John: You authorized vacation? We need everybody working overtime! You don't seem to have backup for anybody. How were you planning to make it through this transition with such thin people resources?

Jack: What kind of planning could I have done in the face of so much uncertainty? How was I to know Marilyn would quit? Progressive is a small company. We only have one person who does each kind of job. We don't have time to take people off line to cross-train, and we can't afford to hire backup for every employee. Furthermore, I didn't know for sure until three weeks ago that this deal was going to fly. I couldn't train people to move up to jobs that didn't even exist. And I certainly couldn't plan vacations around it. Anyway, you told me that computerization would reduce our staffing needs.

John: Eventually it will. But for now it's going to take all our resources to make the transition. This will never work if our employees aren't 100 percent behind it. We're sunk if Ann and your other employees turn out to be as uncommitted as Marilyn.

Jack: I assure you our people are loyal and committed. Talk with Ann. Tell her what we need and that we'll promote her to administrative manager as soon as she has trained someone to take her place. And explain our situation to Harry. Both of them are ambitious and willing to help in a crunch.

John: I hope so. If they aren't, some heads are going to roll. This company cannot grow without people who are willing to change and grow with it. I'll talk to Ann first.

* * *

An hour later, Ann sat in Progressive's employee break room, talking with Connie from the support staff and Harry from customer service. They listened intently as she described her meeting with John.

Ann: I didn't know what the heck was going on. The new guy called me into his office and started lecturing me about how we're all going to have to pull together now that Marilyn's gone.

Connie: What happened to Marilyn? Why did she leave?

Ann: He said she resigned for personal reasons. I think she quit because of all the crazy things they are planning to do.

Harry: What crazy things? I thought things were going to be the same around here—just more customers and more profits.

Ann: Guess again. John thinks he's going to computerize our services . . . in six weeks! You've been through a conversion. Can it be done in six weeks?

Harry: Yeah—if we all work round the clock and don't make the same mistakes my old company did. Of course, nobody has asked for my advice. I don't like them springing this on us at the last minute. We could have started preparing weeks ago if we had known. Now it's going to be a real crunch. And it's too late for me to help. I'm going on vacation at the end of this week.

Ann: Not anymore you aren't. John says all leave is cancelled. He's going to meet with you tomorrow to get your input on installing the system.

Harry: He won't get any input from me. If the management around here doesn't care about my personal plans, I'm not going to bail them out because they were too dumb to make any business plans. They can figure it out for themselves—I quit!

Connie: What about the support staff? What has he planned for us now that Marilyn's gone? We're going to be swamped if we don't get some more help in a hurry!

Ann: I saved the worst for last. We're getting more work, not more help. He wants me to do my job, Marilyn's job, and train someone to take over for me—all at the same time! And he's not even going to replace the person who moves into my job. He bragged about how the computer will reduce our staffing needs, as if I care. My reward for all this will be the administrative manager job, which I don't even want. He said I could move into sales later, when Progressive doesn't have such a critical need for my expertise on the support staff. I don't believe it—you never know what's going to happen around here. I'm sending out my resume today! What about you?

Connie: Me, too. They can find someone else to do their dirty work.

* * *

Growth is painful, stretching people and companies beyond their current limits.

Our story about Progressive illustrates some of the problems that frequently accompany growth. People resist change, particularly the introduction of new management. Top managers become tied up with the details of creating growth and lose touch with the people needed to support it. Valuable employees may leave the company, believing they have been exploited and displaced. Or they may stay on, harboring resentment and working below their potential. *It doesn't have to be this way!*

Three conditions help facilitate successful growth. First, managers and employees must be ready with the competencies to handle growing responsibilities. Second, the people who will implement the changes that accompany business growth must be willing to accept and support those changes. Finally, employees and managers must have the long-term commitment and vision to stick with each other and the company through the short-term discomforts of growth and change.

These conditions require and support the strongest commitment between employees and managers. The next three chapters describe how to develop that kind of deep and enduring commitment as you and your companies grow. Since this is a goal that all working people share, from the CEO to the first-line employee, it will help you to read our recommendations for both managers and employees.

10.

Developing People for Growing Responsibilities

> *"How were you planning to make it through this transition with such thin people resources?"*
>
> *"What kind of planning could I have done in the face of so much uncertainty?"*

The first condition for successful growth is having people in place with the competencies to successfully handle expanded responsibilities.

Commitment weakens when people do not develop at the same rate as the business. Giving employees additional work and responsibilities that they are not ready to handle endangers your company's growth. Bringing in new people who possess the competencies needed creates resentment among employees who believe they were kept in the dark about what they needed to do to grow with the company. Marilyn resented John's intrusion and Jack's failure to give her guidance about her development needs.

In order for people development to keep pace with business development, managers and employees should continually look ahead, forecast, and act on individual development needs. The following suggestions will show you how to do that.

FOR MANAGERS: HOW TO DEVELOP EMPLOYEE COMPETENCIES TO SUPPORT COMPANY GROWTH

DO HUMAN RESOURCE PLANNING AS A PART OF BUSINESS DEVELOPMENT PLANNING.

Map out human resource needs as carefully as you make the financial projections required to back up successful business growth. Although you may not know whether your plans will work out, you do know the general direction in which your business is growing. Systematically consider and act on your answers to the following questions:

1. How is the work content, at the managerial level and below, likely to change as you grow?

2. What kind of special expertise will you need that you do not currently have? How will you get it—from within or by bringing in people from outside? How long will it take to locate and/or train people with the needed expertise?

3. How will your organizational structure and administrative systems change? What will you have to do to make the transition to new structures and systems?

4. What is your succession plan? Large corporations do succession planning as a matter of course. Smaller companies generally don't do formal succession planning in the belief that they don't have enough time or people to do it. The leanness of small companies is the very reason that succession planning is so critical. The loss of one person can create major problems under normal circumstances; during a growth spurt it can be crippling. If you do no other human resource planning, you should at least develop backup for your management team.

Don't wait until the moment your expansion plans will be executed to get the people in place to carry them out. Jack believed there was little planning he could have done until the Competitive deal was a certainty. Two incorrect assumptions supported Jack's failure to adequately plan, assumptions that managers often use to rationalize lack of planning.

The first was that planning is a waste of time when the future is uncertain. If this were true, managers would never plan. The future is always uncertain! A good example of this is Marilyn's unexpected departure. Employees leave suddenly for a variety of reasons: illness, frustrations, other opportunities, relocating spouses, etc. You should do human resource planning *because* the future is uncertain and you never know when you will have to replace a key employee.

Jack's second incorrect assumption was that it is inappropriate to line up people to carry out business plans that may not work out. We suggest the opposite. Mobilizing at the last minute is costly and wasteful and creates unnecessary hardships for managers and employees. If Jack had had the people in position and ready to move and the Competitive deal had fallen through, they would have been ready for the next move. Growing companies don't stop growing because "Plan A" doesn't work out! Eventually Progressive would have utilized the people Jack had developed for expansion.

DEVELOP YOURSELF AND REQUIRE ALL MANAGERS TO DEVELOP THEMSELVES AND THEIR EMPLOYEES.

Plan and act on your own development in ways that are visible and instructive to your employees. Your employees will follow the lead of your example. Jack took no time for his own development. Marilyn followed his lead and did nothing about her own development. Jack bypassed planning Marilyn's development; Marilyn bypassed planning Ann's development.

It's a chain reaction that begins with you. Create a development plan for yourself. Attend management development courses or whatever it is that you need but have been putting off. Help your employees make appropriate development plans for themselves and support them. Make employee development a performance evaluation factor for all employees who supervise others. Your commitment to development will make you and your people keep up with your growing company.

INCLUDE DEVELOPMENT PLANS IN PERFORMANCE EVALUATION.

Performance evaluation is often a backward-looking process. You look at what employees have done over some past period of time, identifying what went well and what did not. If there is any forward focus at all, it is usually in the form of a prescription to correct deficiencies in the performance of an employee's current job. Employees then assume, as Marilyn did, "I'm doing great at my job, and I've been here a long time, so I must be ready to move up."

Not so! It may take entirely different competencies to handle the next job or the next level up in the management hierarchy. You can help employees prepare for that move by prescribing a forward-focused individual development plan that includes the following:

- **Career Goals**

  Although you and your employees may not know exactly what position will come next, you can consider the employee's interests and the organizational possibilities. Obviously you cannot discuss organizational possibilities without first answering the human resource planning questions listed above. In growing companies where the next position does not exist yet, it is particularly important to map out some alternatives with your employees so they can have realistic expectations of what comes next. Marilyn had unrealistic expectations because she and Jack never explored the alternatives.

- **Specific Competency Development Goals and Scheduled Development Activities**

  Such activities may include public seminars and workshops, formal education, an independent study program, or special assignments on the job to help your employees develop new competencies. Help your employees identify and understand how to get from where they are to where they want to be, and coach them along the way.

- **Decision Rules for Moving Up**

  The first decision rule is whether or not your employee has developed the required competencies. An equally important decision rule is the timing of your company's growth. Explain the business factors that will affect the timing and availability of career opportunities. Let your employees know that the business may grow more slowly or more quickly than anticipated and how that will affect their progress. Never let your employees assume, as Marilyn did, that length of service and good performance in their current jobs are the only criteria for promotions. Employees will more readily accept the necessity of bringing in better qualified outsiders if they understand in advance all the criteria for promotion.

When performance evaluation focuses only on past and current performance, employees will be unaware of their development needs and unprepared to move up when they want to and when you are ready for them to move. Planning employee development through performance evaluation shows your commitment to helping your employees grow and succeed with your company.

CROSS-TRAIN ALL EMPLOYEES.

Managers often back up computer systems far better than they back up people systems. No one can afford to lose all the records in a computer system. Yet your employees carry volumes of knowledge and experience around in their heads.

Back up your people. You can give yourself and your company the flexibility to quickly recover from employee losses or to move people around during growth spurts. You can start a comprehensive cross-training program by doing the following:

1. Define the major tasks, employee by employee, of your work unit.

2. Make a list of who knows how to do what. These people are your potential trainers.

3. Make a list of the tasks each person does not know how to do. These are the training needs.

4. Set priorities on the training needs based on where you have the least backup and the most critical functions. The first cross-training should be to teach people to do those tasks that only one person can now do.

5. Make a training schedule for each task so that cross-training occurs at a time when the least possible disruption will result for trainers and trainees.

6. Support the cross-training by honoring the schedule, recognizing trainers and trainees, and participating in it yourself. It never hurts to get a refresher course in what your employees do. Your participation will communicate your commitment to cross-training and employee development.

7. Once employees have covered the major tasks of their own work unit, start a cross-training exchange with the work units that feed into and receive work from yours.

A less comprehensive approach to cross-training is to train two people every time you hire a new employee — i.e., train the new person and one other person at the same time. Or train the new person and let the new person complete his or her own training by teaching the job to a buddy who will be the designated backup. Jack thought cross-training couldn't be done at Progressive because each job was unique and everyone was needed "on line." If you cannot afford to pull anyone off line for training, then you cannot afford *not* to cross-train! Remember also that as more people are cross-trained, more coverage will be available to back up the people involved in training.

Note to Managers: There are three "For Employees" sections in Part III and, as in Part II, we strongly suggest that you review these sections with your employees as part of your career counseling.

FOR EMPLOYEES: HOW TO GROW WITH YOUR COMPANY

DEFINE AND SHARE YOUR CAREER GOALS.

Think through your goals and share them with your manager. Whether you have a specific position in mind or only know the general direction in which you want to go, tell your manager. This is the only way you will find out whether your goals are realistic, how your goals fit with your company's anticipated growth, and what you need to do to reach your goals.

Managers are not mind readers and cannot anticipate what you want and expect. Without knowing your specific aspirations, your manager may assume you will be satisfied with whatever position becomes available. Because Jack did not know what Marilyn expected, he could neither advise her about the feasibility of her goal nor help her get there. The first step toward getting your manager's commitment to the growth you want is to let your manager know what you want!

PLAN YOUR OWN DEVELOPMENT.

After you have defined your career goals and discussed them with your manager, then what? If you are lucky, your manager will make a development plan with you, outlining the competencies you need and identifying development activities to help you acquire those competencies. More likely, your manager may expect you to initiate appropriate development activities.

Rich resources are available for your self-development. Start by investigating the following resources to find out what's available that fits your needs:

- Ask members and leaders of your local or state professional or trade association about development opportunities. Such associations regularly sponsor low- or no-cost development activities for members. Your professional association can also put you in touch with other members who are experts in your area of interest and who may give you their advice and support.

- Talk with coordinators and instructors at local community colleges and universities. Most universities have continuing education programs or extension divisions that offer night or lunchtime classes for working people. Even if you do not need formal courses, instructors in your field can recommend books to read, independent study aids, and people to contact to help you further.

- Ask the manager of a good bookstore what's available in your area. Self-instructional books and tapes are abundant. What you don't see on the shelves can be easily ordered.

- Read! Your manager or the owner of your company probably subscribes to magazines, journals, and newsletters relevant to your industry. Get your name on the circulation list in your office. These publications will include instructional articles as well as advertisements for developmental materials and public seminars that may be of interest to you.

After you have thoroughly checked out what's available, draft a development plan for yourself and give it to your manager for feedback and suggestions. When you show this kind of initiative and commitment to your own development, you make it easier for your manager to respond and support you. You may even lead your manager to invest company time and funds in your development!

LEARN FROM YOUR COWORKERS.

Look in your own backyard. You have an company full of potential trainers available to help you. If your company has a cross-training program, you have an easy route for learning from your coworkers: volunteer for training in the area of your interest. If your company does not have an organized cross-training program, ask your manager to help you identify other employees who possess the competencies you want to develop. Introduce yourself to those employees and ask them for help. Asking them three questions can get you valuable guidance in your development:

1. How did you acquire your skills and experience and how would you suggest I do the same?

2. May I observe you at work and assist you with work that would help me develop new skills?

3. Will you eat lunch with me once a month, listen to me talk about what I'm doing, and give me feedback and suggestions about how I can develop further?

If appropriate, set up a trade whereby you share your time and expertise in exchange for your coworker's time and expertise. Ask your manager to allocate time for your mutual growth. You will be strengthening your company's reserves at the same time you are developing yourselves. Marilyn might have done this with the other middle managers at Progressive and greatly increased the range of her competencies and her promotional opportunities.

DEVELOP YOURSELF TO COMPLEMENT YOUR MANAGER'S SKILLS.

Emulate, don't imitate, your manager. To imitate is to copy — warts and all. To emulate is to try to equal or excel. Learn from your manager's strengths. Develop yourself to compensate for your manager's weaknesses so that you can better serve your manager and your company now and in the future.

Your manager is likely to hire or promote people who can provide the most support, people who can fill in the holes. This is why Jack hired John; John had the formal education in management and experience in a larger company that Jack did not. Marilyn excused herself from formal development, rationalizing that Jack had no credentials either. By imitating Jack, she retarded her own growth and kept herself unqualified for promotion to the position she wanted.

It takes commitment and creativity to emulate your manager. You may not be aware of your manager's deficiencies; your manager may not be aware of them, either. To identify your manager's weaknesses, answer the following questions:

- What characteristics or failings in other people annoy your manager the most? People are frequently intolerant of their own weaknesses when they see them in others! For example, managers who are poor planners often criticize employees for their poor planning skills.

- What kinds of development activity does your manager keep putting off? Jack put off going to the management development program at the local university. Marilyn could have asked for the opportunity and used it to make herself more valuable to Jack and a more viable candidate for future advancement.

- Where is your manager unable to help you?

- Consider how your manager would complete this sentence: "Nobody around here can do _____ worth a damn!" That's an obvious area for you to develop.

Think about these questions and you'll have a good idea of how you should be developing to better support your manager and improve your potential for promotion. Managers value and need employees who can do what they cannot.

11.

Developing Support for Change

> *"This will never work if the employees aren't 100 percent behind it."*
>
> *"They can figure it out for themselves—I quit!"*

The second requirement for successful growth is for employees to actively support the changes accompanying growth.

Unfortunately, resistance is often the response to change, particularly staff and systems changes. Employees may want the company to grow, but may resist new people and new methods that they do not understand or appreciate. The employees at Progressive were elated by the acquisition of Competitive, believing that the only changes would be more customers and more profits. They resisted the necessary intrusion of John and the computer system and reacted by sabotaging the changes. Those who could have done the most to support the growth of Progressive—Marilyn, Ann, and Harry—refused to help and influenced other employees to withhold support, too.

Support for growth and change must be cultivated long before the growth actually occurs, just as gardeners must work the soil, fertilize, weed, and water seedlings before they will produce. The following actions will enable managers and employees to lay the groundwork and develop productive support for change.

FOR MANAGERS: HOW TO CULTIVATE SUPPORT FOR CHANGE

SHARE COMPANY GROWTH POSSIBILITIES WITH EMPLOYEES.

Simply put, employees must understand what's likely to happen in order to support it. You must take the risk of sharing information about what might happen instead of waiting until you know that your plans will work out.

Obviously there are practical limits to sharing information with employees. You don't have time to discuss every possibility. Some plans and possibilities must be kept confidential for business reasons. Here are some practical guidelines on effectively sharing growth plans and possibilities with employees:

- **What to share**

   Share possibilities that will affect the work and work lives of your employees. Share plans that your employees can improve with their criticism and suggested refinements. Share plans that you will depend on your employees to implement.

- **When to share**

   As soon as possible! Unless a deal or a new project must be kept confidential, tell your employees about possibilities as soon as you start acting on them. Your employees will know something is up and will engage in unproductive speculation until you give them enough accurate information to engage in productive thinking and action. The sooner employees know about possibilities, the sooner they can contribute to making those possibilities become positive realities.

- **How much to share**

   Tell your employees enough about possibilities and plans so that they can at least understand the direction and purpose of your company's growth. Give employees enough information to understand the likely implications of your growth plans on their work. When in doubt, share more than you think employees need or want to know. It may take a lot of information to spark employees' interest in and commitment to supporting your growth plans!

• How to share

Routinely share plans and possibilities in regularly scheduled staff meetings at all levels in the company. Occasionally hold "flat" meetings, including top managers, middle managers, supervisors, and employees, to share plans affecting the total company. In addition, top managers can and should informally listen to employees on the line to check their understanding of what's coming up, why, and how it will affect them. This three-pronged approach to communication assures that employees at all levels understand possibilities and plans well enough to stop destructive rumors and support constructive plans. The way *not* to share plans is to circulate a written announcement after the fact and expect employees' immediate understanding and support. People rarely like, understand, or support surprises—even surprises that will be beneficial to them!

You may hesitate to share some plans and possibilities, fearing employee opposition. Possible opposition is a reason in favor of early sharing rather than against it. Withholding information almost always guarantees resistance. You need time to answer objections, reduce employees' natural fears of change, respond to questions and misunderstandings, and let people get used to the idea of a change—all of which can be done only with the greatest difficulty once you reach the implementation stage.

You also want to give your employees time to mobilize most efficiently for supporting the change when the time comes to act. Jack waited until the deal was signed to announce the acquisition of Competitive and the hiring of John Newman; he waited until John's arrival to tell employees about the computerization. As a result, employees at all levels, from Marilyn down the line, were surprised, angry, and resistant. If Jack had shared the possibilities with employees as his plans progressed, he could have gradually built employee acceptance, readiness, and commitment to support the upcoming changes.

INVOLVE EMPLOYEES IN PLANNING THE IMPLEMENTATION OF CHANGES.

Employee commitment to support your company's growth begins when you share information about growth possibilities and plans. Employee support increases when you share responsibility for making the decisions to change and for planning the implementation of changes.

This is not a new idea, but it is one worth repeating. Employee involvement in planning and decision making not only creates commitment, it also creates better decisions and plans! Given enough information and guidance, your employees can help you plan successfully by contributing *their* first-hand knowledge and experience of your company's operations. No matter how creative and experienced you may be, you cannot have the same practical insight into your operations and the effects of potential changes that the people doing the work have. Use their know-how and experience to create better plans at the same time their involvement creates commitment and support for *their* ideas.

Begin involving employees with the kind of information sharing we recommended above. Then, as possibilities become closer to reality, assign individuals and teams of employees to assist you in the information gathering and analysis required to make decisions about changes. Finally, as the decisions for change are agreed upon, assign the employees and work units affected by each decision to plan its implementation.

When employees have been informed and involved throughout the planning process, they will be ready and willing to act on the changes when you are ready to go. And if your growth plans do not work out, you have not wasted your employee's time and energy. Your employees will have gained valuable experience in planning, teamwork, and managing change. You will have a team of supporters ready to go when your contingency plan works out!

The employees at Progressive were uninformed and uninvolved in the decisions for change and the plans for implementing the changes brought on by the acquisition of Competitive. They were committed to Progressive's growth, but they had no opportunity to constructively express and strengthen that commitment. By the time they learned about the changes that would occur, it was too late for them to share their valuable ideas about how to make the changes work. Their exclusion created resentment rather than support for the changes Jack depended upon them to implement.

COMMUNICATE THE DIRECT INDIVIDUAL BENEFITS OF COMPANY GROWTH AND CHANGE.

Never assume that employees will make the connection that what is good for the company is good for them. Employees do not make this connection automatically and often believe that changes mean only more work for them. This belief is frequently based on experience; growth and change usually do create more work—in the short run. Even when employees have been involved in planning changes, you should explain in concrete terms how those changes will directly benefit your employees.

Jack and John described the changes they were introducing at Progressive in terms of benefits to the company. Jack told Marilyn that she needed John's experience and expertise to handle the difficult work ahead. Jack didn't say how John would be able to help Marilyn develop herself to move up to the vice-president position that she wanted. John told Ann that the computer system would reduce Progressive's staffing needs. John didn't say how the computer system would specifically lighten Ann's workload and the work of the other support employees. When you tell employees that a change will help get the work done or will reduce costs and staffing needs, employees will believe that change will benefit managers only. When you introduce a change as an opportunity for employees to get something that they want, your employees will have strong incentive to support the change.

HELP YOUR EMPLOYEES REDUCE THE GROWING PAINS BY WORKING SMARTER.

As we have said before, growth and change create extra work for employees—in the short run. Managers sometimes try to motivate employees to make the extra effort required during a growth spurt by glamorizing the hard work and sacrifice they must make in order for the company to succeed. You know the line: "Only you can pull us through this crunch. Put all other plans on hold and give us all you've got."

Instead of extolling the virtues of hard work, help your employees work smarter and make the change easier. Provide assistance such as temporary employees or specialized business services to handle temporary work overloads. Suggest shortcuts or delays in lower-priority work to lighten the load while implementing changes. Temporarily suspend some time-consuming work rules. Ask employees for their suggestions to ease the burden. Many times they can tell you how to make the change easier if only you will listen.

John tried to solicit employee support for the implementation of the new computer system by telling Ann how much he needed everyone's hard work and by cancelling other employees' vacation plans. Ann and her coworkers responded just as employees often will to do-or-die demands: with passive resistance. The employees knew that the last-minute scrambling and long hours wouldn't have been necessary if they had been involved in the first place, and they resented the unnecessary imposition. They heard nothing from Jack or John to indicate their willingness to reduce the sacrifice required of their employees. Your willingness to support employees through the growing pains creates their willingness to support you.

FOR EMPLOYEES: HOW TO GET SUPPORT DURING GROWTH AND CHANGE

SHOW AN ACTIVE INTEREST IN YOUR COMPANY'S GROWTH POSSIBILITIES AND PLANS.

Managers will respect you and will share information with you about upcoming changes *if* you indicate an interest in your company's growth. Managers don't routinely volunteer information about company growth possibilities because they assume employees aren't interested. Demonstrate your interest in and commitment to supporting your company's growth by doing the following:

- Ask questions and actively participate in staff meetings. Respond positively when your manager presents information about current business status and plans. For example, your manager might share summaries of quarterly sales, budget, production, or some other form of company progress report with you. If you remain silent during and after the presentation, your manager may assume you are uninterested. Ask questions if you don't understand the meaning or implications of the information presented. Ask how your company's current status will affect future growth. Ask what causes sales increases/declines and whether your product or service mix will likely change as a result. Ask what budget allocations mean, particularly significant shifts of funds to capital or development accounts. Ask your manager whether your company is preparing for growth and what that growth will likely be. Respond to the information your manager gives you, and your manager will respond to you.

- Volunteer for task forces or other employee groups that are working on improving operations or making the company a better place to work. Your participation shows your commitment to your company's current and future success and puts you in a setting where you can learn and contribute to growth and change plans.

- Specifically tell your manager that you want to hear about growth and change possibilities and support them in any way you can. Remember that some employees avoid change and prefer stability; your manager will not know that *you* value growth and change unless *you* say so.

Don't excuse yourself from knowing about upcoming growth or changes by saying that nobody told you. Your manager can as easily use the excuse that nobody asked. Harry was angry that he did not know about the computer system in time to get ready. Yet he knew about the acquisition of Competitive and did not ask the simple and obvious questions: "What kind of changes will all this new business create in our work? What can I do now to prepare for the new business?"

SUPPORT GROWTH AND CHANGE AMONG YOUR COWORKERS.

Spread the word about the positive effects of growth and change. Regardless of the specific kind of growth or change your company is undergoing, there are some indisputable benefits of growth. A successful growing company is the best kind of job security. Few companies can remain successful if they do not change to meet changing market needs and surpass growing competitors.

Employees who stonewall changes appear uncommitted to company success even when their concerns are motivated by a genuine belief that the change will be detrimental to the company. Rather than complain in public, discuss your concerns in private with your manager. Ask your manager to help you understand the benefits of the change. Discuss those benefits with your coworkers. If you do, your manager will see you as a committed and promotion-worthy employee. If you resist the way Ann and her coworkers did, you will be seen as a troublemaker and treated accordingly. John's plan for employees who resisted the changes at Progressive was that "heads would roll." Many managers employ John's strategy, knowing that a company cannot grow without employees who are willing to grow with it.

FACILITATE THE IMPLEMENTATION OF CHANGE.

To facilitate change is to make it easier. The best way to make change easier is to put your creative energies into making the change work as soon as you hear about it, even if you don't hear about it until the last minute.

Again, it is no excuse to say that nobody asked for your ideas. Nobody knows you have any ideas until you start sharing them. Keeping silent when you know how to facilitate implementation and avoid problems is sabotage. To facilitate the implementation of change, follow these guidelines:

- Support change among your coworkers. Help other employees understand the benefits of change.

- Be an informal leader among your coworkers. Voice the concerns and fears of others to your manager for the purpose of problem-solving, not griping. This gives your manager the opportunity to address those concerns and help everyone work more effectively.

- Volunteer to work extra if needed. Your manager will be working as long and hard as you and can't afford to waste time forcing reluctant employees to help out in a crisis.

- Share all information you have about what will and will not work. Don't knowingly allow the implementation to be harder than it has to be. If you do, you are only punishing yourself, because it's your time that will be wasted in working inefficiently.

WORK SMART AND ASK FOR HELP!

No matter how well you and your manager prepare for growth, it inevitably requires hard work. Be willing to work hard and think creatively about how to work efficiently. Suggest shortcuts and labor-savers. Stop and take the time to plan the best way to get everything done instead of planning to work nonstop until everything is done. Check frequently with your manager about priorities so that you apply your energy to the most important tasks. Be assertive about asking your manager for extra help instead of complaining to your coworkers about not having enough help. Your assertiveness and creativity will show your commitment to getting the job done and will give your manager a chance to respond to your needs.

Ann and Connie never considered the possibility of proposing ways in which John could help them. They expected him to think through their workload problems and take care of them. A new manager like John, or even a manager who has been in place for a long time, cannot think of all the ways to ease the burden of change. Managers depend on you to tell them what you need to work most efficiently.

12.

Developing Lasting Commitment

> *"I thought she was my most loyal employee."*
>
> *"We're sunk if Ann and your other employees turn out to be as uncommitted as Marilyn."*

The third requirement for successful growth is mutual long-term commitment between managers and employees. It takes such commitment to stick together through the growing pains and to build a profitable long-living company. When such commitment does not exist, turnover occurs and managers and employees must begin again the long and costly process of starting over with a new employee or a new job.

Long-term commitment cannot be created in the middle of a growth spurt. Commitment begins the moment a manager and a prospective employee shake hands. It either grows or diminishes through your daily actions and interactions.

Every action we have recommended in this book thus far will help you build enduring mutual commitment. Our remaining suggestions will strengthen and reinforce what you have been learning how to do all along. These final recommendations are not something to look up and start practicing when your company starts growing; they are the capstone for working together to create caring relationships that will withstand the tests of time and change.

FOR MANAGERS: HOW TO BUILD ENDURING MUTUAL COMMITMENT

CREATE A SATISFYING PRESENT AND A REWARDING FUTURE FOR YOUR EMPLOYEES.

Make each day at work a satisfying experience that contributes to a rewarding future for your employees. The two vehicles for doing this are daily recognition of your employees' value and your strong commitment to providing concrete future rewards for your employees.

Daily recognition of your employees' importance and contributions creates a satisfying present. Jack waited until the end of a long successful project to praise and recognize his most valued employee. Then he tarnished that recognition with a plea for more hard work! If you do as Jack did, your employees will feel as Marilyn did: unappreciated and manipulated. An infrequent pat on the back cannot make up for months of silence.

In addition to giving your employees daily recognition, commit to concrete future rewards. It is only when you do both that your employees will believe in and reciprocate your long-term commitment. Concrete future rewards include retirement, savings, or stock option programs; graduated salary increases for sustained excellent performance; and active commitment to employee development and career plans. A one-time bonus at the end of a special project provides immediate gratification but offers little incentive for sustained performance or commitment. Your employees must know that you are committed to rewarding them over the long haul in order to be committed over the long haul. Jack made no such commitment to Marilyn and she in turn made no such commitment to him.

STAY IN TOUCH WITH EMPLOYEES' FEELINGS.

Many of the recommendations in this book have focused on clearly communicating information about work activities and purposes. We have emphasized that when you carefully share information with your employees, you are showing your commitment to helping them understand and succeed in their work. While this is true, an equally important aspect of communicating with your employees is staying in touch with their feelings. By this we mean going beyond telling people what to do to listening to how they feel about doing it. In order for your employees to know that you truly care about them and are committed to their long-term welfare, you must acknowledge and respond to their feelings as well as their thinking.

For many people, communicating at a feeling level is uncomfortable and frightening. When Jack told Marilyn about her new job and her new boss, he could see the unhappiness on her face. Instead of letting her talk about it, he tried to quickly smooth over her discomfort by telling her to take some time off to get herself together. He dismissed Marilyn's feelings as something to be worked out on her own, which she did by acting on them and deciding to resign. Although the consequences of being out of touch with your employees' feelings are not always so extreme, the inevitable consequences are reduced commitment and work effectiveness.

Getting and staying in touch with feelings requires mutual openness and trust. There's no formula for creating openness and trust, but you can create positive conditions for sharing feelings by doing the following:

- Spend some unstructured one-on-one time with each employee you directly supervise at least once a week. This could be lunch, a coffee break, driving together to a meeting, or chatting before or after work. Use this time to initiate personal communication rather than task-oriented discussion. Describe how you *feel* about something. You might share that you are worried about (or proud of) how your kids are doing in school, or that you had a lot of fun playing tennis last weekend, or that you are feeling overwhelmed with all the work you have to do. It doesn't really matter what you say as long as you let your employee know that you value and will share feelings. If you do this regularly, your employees will see you as an open person and will respond by being open with you.

- In task-oriented discussions with your employees, routinely ask how they feel about the task at hand or about the information they have just heard. The simple question "How do you feel about this?" can open the door for meaningful sharing that will increase your employees' commitment to the task and to you.

- Provide structured opportunities in group meetings for you and your employees to bring up and explore the personal dimensions of work life. For example, before you address any of the agenda items at your staff meetings, ask each person to talk about how they are feeling about important things going on with them in their jobs. The first few times you do this, you may have to start it off and model how you want your employees to be: open, honest, and vulnerable. Talk about what you are happy about. Talk about your fears. Talk about where you need "moral support." Doing this invites your employees to do the same.

• Be a *listener*. In every exchange with your employees, try to spend more time listening than talking. Ask for your employees' feelings and opinions and hear them out. Allow plenty of time for important discussions instead of saying your piece and running off to the next meeting. Look at your employees when they are talking to you and concentrate on what they are saying. Don't make your To Do list, check your in-basket, take phone calls, or do anything else but listen when an employee is talking with you. Your listening communicates respect and commitment to your employee.

If Jack had stayed in touch with his employees in these ways, they could have developed the commitment needed to make it through Progressive's growth spurt. He might have told them that he was frightened at the prospect of successfully handling so much new business, that he was worried about his own inexperience and lack of education for managing a larger enterprise, and that he needed more help and support. Marilyn might have shared her disappointment about his bringing in a new vice-president. The other employees, in their turn, might have shared their confusion, fears, and anger at having to install the computer system on such short notice. Without this kind of sharing, they were unable to understand, support, or commit to one another for the present or the long run.

TALK ABOUT THE FUTURE AND YOUR EMPLOYEES' PLACES IN IT.

Show commitment to your employees by letting them know they are your company's future. Sharing possibilities and plans is a part of this, and so is employee development. In addition, talk generally about how you and your employees are building a shared future. Describe what you foresee for your company, not six months ahead, but many years down the road. Talk about how large your company may grow; how your products or services may further specialize or broaden; whether your company will continue to be a local business or expand regionally or nationally; how your company will be structured and managed, and so forth. Ask your employees how they would like the company to be in the future and invite them to contribute their ideas for getting there. Listen to your employees' life plans and aspirations and explore with them how they can fulfill their dreams as part of your company. Give them a vision to commit to and build with you so they will have good reason to hang in there with you when the going gets tough.

Our friends at Progressive apparently had no such discussions. Marilyn, Ann, and their coworkers couldn't see beyond the immediate hardships of growth and the disappointments of today. Jack saw them all in the future of Progressive, but he did not share that future with them by talking about it and involving them in it.

ASSUME THAT YOUR EMPLOYEES CARE, AND RESPOND TO THEM ACCORDINGLY.

This is the assumption upon which our book is based and the assumption upon which you must consistently act if you and your employees are going to develop mutual long-term commitment: *People will conform to your expectations.*

To appreciate the power of your beliefs about employees, think about how you respond to employees when you assume that they don't care about you, your company, or their work. You probably respond with controls, criticism, and demands. After all, you wouldn't give important responsibilities, support, and choices to uncommitted employees. Now think about how *you* respond to controls, criticism, and demands. Your individual responses may vary, but the universal responses are resistance and rejection—the opposite of commitment.

Our assumption is a self-fulfilling prophecy. When you assume your employees are committed, you will behave toward them in the constructive ways we have outlined in this book. You will give them responsibilities, support, and choices. And they will inevitably give you their commitment.

We wrote this book for you because you may unconsciously tell your employees that you are uncommitted to them and you believe they are uncommitted to you by the actions and inactions we described in the stories at the beginning of each chapter. In our final story, Jack and John subtly and unintentionally expressed a profound disbelief in their employees' commitment. Jack ignored Marilyn's daily contributions and hard work, made no concrete commitment to her future, hired a new boss for her without telling her what was coming or why, hid his own feelings and discounted hers, and, worst of all, accepted her resignation second-hand without following her out the door to prevent the loss of his supposedly most valued employee. Jack sent the same message to his other employees by withholding information about the upcoming changes, giving them no opportunity to react to or give input in the changes, and failing to share a vision of the future with them.

As we have said repeatedly, it doesn't have to be this way! If you really believe and act as if your employees are committed, they will be. They will be because you will make them so by your leadership.

FOR EMPLOYEES: HOW TO CREATE ENDURING MUTUAL COMMITMENT

WORK FOR FUTURE REWARDS IN THE PRESENT.

The way to get your manager's commitment to giving you the future you want is to commit yourself to fulfilling your manager's present need. It's trite but true that you can't have it all now. You must give your best effort where it is needed today so that your manager and your company will be able to provide the rewards you want tomorrow.

Marilyn and Ann both wanted positions that did not fit with their manager's present need. Marilyn wanted a position that required greater competencies than she possessed and was unwilling to support the person who needed her help and could have helped her develop those competencies. Ann wanted a position for which she was marginally qualified and rejected a position where her competencies were most desperately needed. They both would have gotten what they wanted if they had been willing to do what was necessary to put their company and their manager in a position to provide it.

The best expression of your long-term commitment is your willingness to serve *now*. When you help your manager create a successful future, you are creating your manager's commitment to a successful future for you.

SHARE YOUR FEELINGS WITH YOUR MANAGER INSTEAD OF ACTING THEM OUT WITH YOUR COWORKERS.

A sure sign of your commitment is your willingness to share your feelings about what's happening at work with your manager. Some people think you should share only positive feelings with your manager and save your negative feelings for your friends in the break room. No positive results can come from these gripe sessions, and a great deal of harm can come from undermining other employees' commitment.

Ann saw herself as a committed employee, yet she ran straight from John to tell her coworkers about all the injustices John was about to propagate. By doing this, she practically ensured the failure of the computer system implementation and John's failure as a manager at Progressive. In the process, she gained nothing for herself but company in her misery, along with the likelihood that John would fire her before she had the chance to find another job.

A far more constructive and courageous response would have been to be honest with John about her feelings and, if she got no response from him, to share her feelings with Jack. She robbed them both of the opportunity to address and allay her own anger and fears and those of her coworkers.

Express your negative feelings to the person who can do something about them. Most managers will tell you they would much rather hear about your feelings directly than to have to deal with the domino effect of indirect complaints. Managers appreciate and trust employees who support them by telling them the bad news. When you are committed enough to be honest with your manager, your manager will be committed to supporting you.

TALK ABOUT YOUR VISION OF THE FUTURE AND YOUR PLACE IN IT.

Show your commitment by talking about your future in the company. You might begin with your next career goal, but you need to do more than that to make yourself a part of your manager's vision of the future. Ask your manager to tell you about your company's long-term goals and plans. Tell your manager you want to be an active contributor and not just a passive observer along the way. Share your own plans and goals—life plans, not just what you want two years down the road. Talk about how the company's future fits with those plans.

We have already observed that neither Jack nor his employees initiated this kind of discussion. If Ann or Marilyn had, they could have learned a lot about Progressive's future and painted a clear picture in Jack's mind of themselves as leaders of the future. Their silence left him seeing them mainly in the present picture, with only vague plans for their future development. Although he was committed to them both, he might have been more actively committed to fulfilling their aspirations, and fulfilling them sooner, if they had shown an active interest in the future of Progressive.

BELIEVE IN YOUR MANAGER'S COMMITMENT TO YOU AND ACT ACCORDINGLY.

Our message to managers about the power of assumptions and self-fulfilling prophecies holds true for employees, too. If you act as if your manager were uncommitted, with resistance and rebellion, your manager will soon be as uncommitted as you believe. If you act as if your manager were committed to you, with support, cooperativeness, and responsibility, your manager will be committed to you.

We wrote this book for employees, not just for managers, because employees have as much power as managers to create commitment and a satisfying work life for themselves. Ann often believed that Marilyn and Jack weren't committed to her, and her ways of responding to them had the result of reducing their commitment. In our final scene, Ann took actions that could only end the commitment of Progressive's managers to her. She turned the other employees against the change required to make Progressive grow successfully. If she had acted instead out of the belief that her manager was committed to her and had supported John and the implementation of the computer system, she could have earned herself a permanent place among the leaders of the company. All along Ann had the power to create commitment for herself, if only she had believed such commitment existed.

That's a radical concept. *You have the power to create a satisfying work life and commitment for yourself.* Most of our suggestions to you have told you how to do for yourself what managers might be expected to do for you—if they were perfect organizers, perfect communicators, and perfect leaders. We haven't met a perfect manager yet, and you don't have to have a perfect manager to get the commitment and rewards you want. Believe in your managers and help them express their commitment to you. You are the essential ingredient in creating a company that cares. Give it your best shot and you'll get as much as you give.

* * *

Part Three: Summary

Three conditions must exist to ensure successful growth. Managers and employees must be ready with the competencies to handle increased responsibilities. Managers and employees who will implement the changes resulting from growth must be willing to accept and support those changes. Finally, employees and managers must have the long-term commitment and vision to stay together through the growing pains.

To develop employees' capacities to handle business growth, managers can begin by doing human resource planning as a part of business development planning. Then employees and managers can together set realistic career goals and map out development plans to meet those goals. Managers should set an example by developing themselves and by requiring their employees to develop themselves and the people they supervise. Managers should also routinely cross-train employees. Employees can develop themselves by emulating their managers and by learning from their coworkers.

Support for change begins with information and involvement. Managers should share growth possibilities and plans, involve employees in decision making and planning the implementation of change, and communicate the direct benefits of change to employees. Managers should also help employees work smart to reduce the pain of implementing change. Employees can show support for growth and change by expressing interest in growth plans, advocating change among their coworkers, facilitating the implementation of change, and working smart to reduce the growing pains.

Long-term commitment grows from daily interactions between managers and employees. Managers should make both the present and the future satisfying and rewarding, stay in touch with employees' feelings, talk about the future and employees' places in it, and believe in their employees' commitment. Employees should work for future rewards with present commitment, share their feelings, talk about the future, and believe in their managers' commitment.

Afterword: "Yes, but . . . "

The assumption behind this book is that most managers and employees really do care, that you are committed to one another, and that you want to work together to create mutual satisfaction and success for your companies. We have asked you to accept, believe, and act on that assumption, and we have told you that if you do, you will get the commitment you want.

Unfortunately, some of you will try our suggestions and will not get the commitment you want. Your response to us will be, "Yes, this all sounds great in theory, but that's not the way it works at my company, or with my manager, or with my problem employees. So what do I do now?"

First, you try again. Time and again restate your intentions and follow our suggestions. If you have just begun consciously and deliberately to express your commitment and to believe in the commitment of others, you will experience some initial failures. People will continue to respond to you in the same ways in which they did before. They will test your commitment until they have changed their own beliefs about you! It takes time and persistence on your part to pass the test and effectively demonstrate that you mean what you say.

Then, if your response is still "Yes, but . . . ," our final suggestion is to end the relationship. This may seem like a strange suggestion in a book about commitment, but separation can also be an expression of commitment.

For managers, firing those employees who do not commit and make a positive contribution to the company is an expression of commitment to those employees who do. Few actions by managers reduce morale and commitment more than allowing disruptive, nonperforming employees to remain on the payroll. Managers also support the people they dismiss by removing them from a situation that is unsatisfying and unrewarding. When a genuine mismatch occurs and employees either don't like work or the work environment, everyone benefits from separation.

For employees, leaving a work situation where you aren't getting the satisfaction and commitment you want is the ultimate expression of caring and responsibility for yourself. Be sure to follow our suggestions beginning in the employment interviews for your next job. Eventually you will find work and a work environment that you can support and will support you.

If you take this final suggestion, don't generalize from an exception that our basic assumption and our suggestions for expressing commitment don't work. They do. We have seen it happen. We want it to happen for you.

About the Authors

Michael C. Thomas is a senior trainer and consultant with Farr Associates, Inc., of Greensboro, North Carolina. His consulting practice focuses primarily on leadership development, employee commitment, team building, and self-managing teams. He has helped managers and employees work together as teams in a number of industries including manufacturing, construction, retail, wholesale, health care, banking, insurance, and professional services. He holds a Ph.D. from the University of North Carolina at Chapel Hill.

Tempe S. Thomas is an educator and a writer. She specializes in educational and human resource management topics.

O • R • D • E • R • F • O • R • M

Please send me **Getting Commitment at Work: A Guide For Managers and Employees.** ISBN 0-9623266-0-7 **$12.95**

Quantity		Unit Price	Amount
	Shipping & Handling ($2.00 First Book) 50¢ each Additional Book		
	Applicable Sales Tax (North Carolina residents only - 5%)		
	TOTAL		

DISCOUNT SCHEDULE

(Save on Quantity Orders)

1 - 5	$12.95
6 - 19	$11.95
20 - 99	$10.95
100+	$ 9.95

MAIL ORDER FORM TO

COMMITMENT PRESS
P.O. Box 2363
Chapel Hill, NC 27515-2363

or Call TOLL FREE

(800) 752-2471

NAME _____

ORGANIZATION _____

ADDRESS _____

CITY _____ STATE _____ ZIP _____

PHONE (_____) _____

❏ Payment Enclosed ❏ MC [MasterCard] ❏ VISA [VISA]

Card # _____ Exp. Date _____

A-1 Signature _____